INTENTIONAL
LEADERSHIP
IN BETWEEN SEASONS

INTENTIONAL
LEADERSHIP

IN BETWEEN SEASONS

SARAH B. DRUMMOND

the pilgrim press

The Pilgrim Press, 1300 East 9th Street
Cleveland, Ohio 44114
thepilgrimpress.com

Published 2022.

Scripture quotations, unless otherwise noted, are from the New Revised Standard Version of the Bible, © 1989 by the Division of Christian Education of the National Council of Churches of Christ in the United States of America. Used by permission. Changes have been made for inclusivity.

Printed on acid-free paper.

26   25   24   23   22   1   2   3   4   5

Library of Congress Cataloging-in-Publication Data on file.
LCCN: 2022932291

ISBN 978-0-8298-0016-6 (alk. paper)
ISBN 978-0-8298-0017-3 (ebook)

Printed in The United States of America.

DEDICATION

For

Jacqueline Judith "JJ" Drummond,

*who teaches me that the present is
a wonderful place to be and gives me
reasons to look with hope to the
leaders of the future.*

CONTENTS

INTRODUCTION

S ewing, for me, started out as an ordinary quarantine project. I had long owned a sewing machine and wanted to learn how to use it. In the past, I had made halfhearted attempts to find online courses or workshops at fabric stores, but I was fairly sure I would learn best by doing. One obstacle stood between me and the doing, however: I did not know how to thread the sewing machine.

The instruction manual seemed to have been written for those who already knew how to thread a sewing machine but had forgotten a detail or two. My mind went to Robert Pirsig's *Zen and the Art of Motorcycle Maintenance*,[1] where the narrator wrote instruction manuals, finding the discipline of providing clear instructions to be satisfying in that it cleansed him of assumptions. I wanted an assumption-cleansed user's guide for my sewing machine. When the Covid-19 pandemic began in earnest, and the reality that it would not end quickly began to settle in, I decided to conquer the threading dilemma so I could teach myself how to sew. I needed to produce something tangible, feeling as helpless as we all did in those months.

I started and gave up three times before I successfully threaded the machine. Small victories included my daughter, then seventeen, taking one look at the manual and machine and showing me a section of the upper mechanism where I had wrapped the thread in the wrong place. And my mother telling me over the phone that a problem I was having might have resulted from the bobbin in the lower thread having been placed the wrong way around. I learned a little by trial and error, a little through patience, and sometimes I wanted to give up.

The real breakthrough happened when I came to understand the essential nature of tension in the functioning of a sewing machine. No one had told me that getting the tension just right between the upper and lower threads was the name of the game. The reason the upper thread goes through channel after channel, giving it abundant opportunities to become tangled or threaded wrongly, is to create just enough tension to keep the thread from flying off the top spool. The lower thread's bobbin case is loaded like a spring, and a tiny screw controls how tense or loose that spring will be. I had to figure out on my own that balancing tension was the whole point of the complexity of a sewing machine. Balanced tension became a central metaphor of long months of self-isolation.

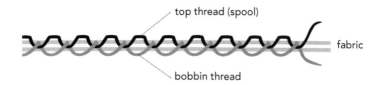

top thread (spool)

fabric

bobbin thread

Figure 1: Machine-Sewn Seams

The diagram above[2] suggests that the intentional leader pays attention at both ends of the thread, setting the sewing machine so that threads resist each other with equal force, gently yet firmly. When a sewing machine is threaded properly, the person sewing can change directions constantly and creatively, stitching a seam or embroidering a design. Linearity is no longer necessary. The tight perfection of the stitches does not relate to where they are going, but how they are finding the proper pull against one another. We only know we have gotten the tension right when the stitches are neat and even, viewed from both the top and the bottom. Similarly, we know we have found the right tensions in our life by a sense of balance, coupled with the energy that comes from striving for that balance.

Throughout most of my life, my relationship with time was linearly forward-leaning. Peter J. Gomes, longtime preacher to Harvard University, described Christians as "a future people." By his definition, I was an excellent Christian. Goal-oriented and self-disciplined, the next moment was a more comfortable place for me to think about than the current one. A lot of good things happened to me due to a future-leaning relationship with time, but my moments of happiness did not take place when I was thinking about what would come next. The real joy was in moments of presence, the rare occasions when I was not looking at the time, or if I was looking at the time, I was wishing time would stop rather than give way to what was next. Our future is beyond our control. Living in the future, therefore, is a setup for disappointment and disorientation.

Two major events in my life took place in the academic year 2019–2020 that caused me to befriend time in a new way. I started a new position that felt, for the first time, like a landing place. Being appointed and beginning in my role as Founding Dean of Andover Newton Seminary at Yale Divinity School was a culmination, rather than one more step toward something else. Every word of the position's title felt like a fulfillment.

- Founding: I had always dreamed of starting something new, but I love tradition so much that I did not think it could happen. Andover Newton, a 214-year-old theological school, became embedded in Yale University, a 350-year-old university; so two old institutions came together to create something new.

- Dean: career assessment testing has told me—if life experience had not been persuasive enough—that educational administration is a natural state of being for me. I love students, I love learning, and I love the challenge that comes with keeping the proverbial trains running on time while also building a life-giving community.

- Seminary: ministry and the Christian faith are essential to my values and identity. I understand myself to be a minister, and my context is schools. Therefore, a school that focuses on educating clergy brings together who I am, that about which I care, and what I like to do.

When I was installed as Andover Newton at Yale Divinity School's Founding Dean, I had worked for twenty-five years in ministry and education, but throughout that time, I had blended different professional roles to find the right balance, always wondering if the future would hold a role that could bring my multiple identities together. Who knows how long it will last, or how I will do, but even knowing that it is possible to find a position where I could imagine working for the rest of my working days felt like a discovery and a reorientation to time. My longed-for professional future is now.

The second reorienting event of 2019–2020 was the Covid-19 pandemic. As I write this introduction, it is very much underway.

In the Covid-19 pandemic, I and so many others changed our lives dramatically. We do not know how long the pandemic will last, but it, like my new professional role, has upended my relationship with time. I cannot derive energy from busyness, even though I am busy. I have to pace myself differently and find interior sources of motivation. My colleagues and I have had to rethink everything we do. Rethinking exposes our habits of mind. One of the habits I can now see clearly is my propensity to lean into a future that has now been exposed in its imaginariness.

I am sure I am not alone in having to rethink what motivates me and find new sources of inspiration during this uncertain time. One of my great professional joys is in academic advising. This fall, I have found myself in at least three conversations with advisees who are ardent planners, in need of something to plan. One wanted to get more involved in the life of our school outside the classroom, but with no gatherings permitted, she needed to find some methodical way of learning her options. I helped her create something that felt like a plan so she would have something on which to focus. Two other advisees described feeling like they, as first-year graduate students, should have a solid sense of what they want to do after they graduate, yet they are in the midst of programs that call for ongoing discernment, not a signed, sealed, and delivered goal. So, I put them on a regimen, too, and gave them to-do lists so that they would not feel so lost in a time when all seems up in the air.

What good was a forward-leaning posture doing for me to the extent that I relied on it for most of my professional (and—who are we kidding?—personal) life? I am coming to realize that it was providing the kind of energy that results from tension. What do I mean by "energy that results from tension"? Consider the exercise regime of astronauts in orbit. Because they cannot rely on gravity to provide resistance, their muscles risk atrophy. Therefore, as I learned in elementary school in the 1970s, when all were fascinated by the space program, they perform isometric exercises. For instance, they would join their hands in front of them and pull their hands against one another, giving their shoulder muscles the needed resistance to strain so they could stay strong.

Resistance requires our energy, and over time, it becomes what we rely upon to get strong and stay energized. Most of us were trained to believe that resistance results from striving into the future. When that future is nebulous and uncertain, however, it makes for an unsatisfying plumb line. We must find resistance within ourselves. We can reproduce the energizing tension that comes from our response to resistance without relying on a goal, something to which we aspire "out there" in an imaginary future. We can build resistance into daily living by cultivating and nurturing the opposing forces that shape our daily lives.

So far, I have described the beginnings of a new leadership theory based on the insights that:

- Striving toward a goal energizes us.
- Goal-orientation changes over the course of a lifetime, and from generation to generation.
  - I personally am at a point in my life when out-there-in-the-future goals are unhelpful.
  - Our society, in the midst of what leadership consultant and author Susan Beaumont and others call "liminality,"[3] is similarly unable to find great inspiration from a goal in a future that is nebulous and unknown.

■ It is possible to reproduce the energizing effects of goal-orientation through tension—not unlike the tension that a sewing machine injects into two threads by pulling them against one another—as a means of finding life-giving motivation in a liminal season.

Many people seeking happiness and sustainability in their lives strive to find balance. The word "balance" suggests a state of equilibrium and all its pleasing results: mental clarity, peaceful relationships, physical wellbeing.

I suggest that tension can serve as an energizing force for motivation and direction, but I do not equate tension with "balance." Tension is similar to balance in that two forces counter each other to ultimately put us in the center. Balance describes the end point, not the practice that led us there, however. In this book, I will use the expression "balancing tension," but I mean that term in the most active possible sense.

We cultivate tension to find a balance.

Certainly, balance has its critics. I have been one of those critics during demanding seasons in my life, when the idea of finding a balance between work and play, or striving and submission, seemed laughable. I was not able to find balance on a daily basis as a new, working parent, for example. That also was a season in my life when every time I heard someone extol the virtues of balance, I felt like I had failed at one more thing. Having my shortcomings in balancing action and reflection, or work and rest, pointed out to me—often by those at different points in their lives where rest was more feasible—felt like getting beaten when I was already down.

Like with so many dimensions of leadership, we hear many scolding messages about where we should have arrived but receive little instruction on how to get there. We are told not to triangulate or get triangulated, but no one tells us how to get out of the middle without seeming indifferent or uninvested. We are told to set healthy boundaries, but doing so is not a passive maneuver. What actions, then, does a person with healthy boundaries take to achieve separate-yet-togetherness?

The title of this book is a play on words. We seek to arrive at a state of balanced tensions, and in order to live in tension, we need *in*tention to get there. In-tension-al leadership is a preferred state of being to goal-oriented leadership, because it does not rely on arriving at particular goals in a future time during a cultural season when "arrival" at equilibrium is an impossibility. We cultivate tensions not just to find balance, but to find the energy resource that goals might once have provided. Balance is a pleasing side effect of finding a healthy tension that keeps us motivated without giving too much of our leadership satisfaction over to circumstances beyond our control.

Since this book is primarily concerned with communal leadership, it will focus on the five tensions that I believe are hardest to maintain in the role of the authorized leader in the context of a group of people seeking a common purpose. Without further ado, here are the tensions that present the most challenge and thus the most fascinating complexities:

Tension 1: Individuality – Community
Tension 2: Inclusivity – Clear identity
Tension 3: Planning – Nimbleness
Tension 4: Affiliative leadership – Authoritative leadership
Tension 5: Structure – Creativity

The book is broken up into two broad sections: first, a theoretical foundation for in-tension-al, intentional leadership, then, a second section describing the five tensions in their theoretical nature and practical implications. In the conclusion, I will present a fictional case and analyze it using the tensions as a guide for understanding the situation and choosing a path of action.

The past three years have presented leadership crises, one after the other: Covid-19, contentious elections, racial reckoning, an economy unmanageable for those with the fewest resources, and the specter of environmental catastrophe looming around the corner. To write a book about good, healthy, compassionate, and life-giving leadership will surely feel at times like playing Nero's violin, but I would rather think of it as a spiritual practice of choosing optimism, choosing hope, and choosing to believe that leadership can be done well—and will be in our lifetimes. For that preferred leadership future to come to pass, help is needed in the form of theoretical frameworks that transcend present circumstances and redefine excellence in such a way that "excelling" no longer means making headway toward a constantly moving target, but rather spurs us to outdo our own best efforts in the pursuit of effectiveness, impact, and goodness.

NOTES

1. Robert M. Pirsig, *Zen and the Art of Motorcycle Maintenance: An Inquiry into Values* (New York: Morrow Quill, 1979).

2. "Hand Stitching vs. Machine Stitching," Robes de Coeur, last modified January 13, 2020, https://www.robesdecoeur.com/blog/hand-stitching-vs-machine -stitching.

3. Susan Beaumont, *How to Lead When You Don't Know Where You're Going: Leading in a Liminal Season* (Lanham, MD: Rowman & Littlefield, 2019).

PART ONE

In Between Times

I have taught leadership theory to seminary students for sixteen years, beginning immediately after completing doctoral studies on that topic. When I began that work, I described to students the flow from the modern to the postmodern eras, and how the challenge of postmodernity for institutions lay in the fact that they were built upon modernist assumptions and structures. Whereas the modern era, typified by the Industrial Revolution and post–Second World War civilization building, followed certain predictable if unjust rules, postmodernity opened up societies to more variety and thus (sometimes welcome) chaos.

More recently, I have had to account for post-postmodernity, where the opening up of postmodernity has also led to reclaiming of certain forms of closedness, which some call "new tribalism." I am beginning to realize that I have to change yet again. Something more is happening in the primordial soup that is post-postmodernity. Something new is emerging, but not yet. Something is gestating, but we may not live to see it born. How can we even begin to think about leadership in such a time as this? The chapters that follow will analyze the question—how do we lead in between seasons?—to which I propose intentional leadership might be one of the answers.

■ 1 ■

DEFINING LEADERSHIP

During my undergraduate and Master of Divinity studies, I was not aware that a field of inquiry on leadership existed. Business? Public policy? Sure. But "leadership" seemed part of other fields, not one unto itself. In retrospect, leadership is all I ever wanted to study, but all I thought I could do was get close to the topic, without any direct access. I thought I could approach it asymptotically through other fields, and of course I thought most leadership was learned on the job. In many ways, I was right. Leadership is multidisciplinary and best learned in conjunction with reflective practice.

I earned a Bachelor of Arts with a major in Ethics, Politics, and Economics; those three disciplines have everything to do with leadership. I then earned a Master of Divinity, which digs a deep, theological well for leadership meaning-making. Concurrently with all those experiences, I was, of course, learning leadership on the job. After the Master of Divinity program, I took a ministry position that came with the responsibility of supervising student ministers. I took a course on supervision, and in it, every participant had the chance to choose one book to read and share with the class. I chose Ronald Heifetz's *Leadership without Easy Answers,*[4] and it changed everything for me.

Heifetz showed me the role leaders play in guiding communities through change, which stood in stark contrast to my previously held belief that, as long as a decision was right (or, truthfully, as long as *I* was right), leaders could and should push it through. My formation as a human being—from my family life to my formal education, from practicing athletics to practicing arts—had taught me to rely on a combination of reason and hard work. Bringing a community along gradually toward a more life-giving way, decentering reason, and opening up to different ways of making sense of the world had a catalytic effect on my thinking, my relationships, and even my faith.

Heifetz's leadership theories are, by now, so familiar to me that I draw on them daily. The three concepts with which he works that I have found most relevant to ministerial leadership include balcony versus dance-floor thinking; technical versus adaptive change; and, more recently, new hope for incrementalism.

Balcony versus dance-floor thinking. Heifetz uses the image of a dance hall with a balcony to describe the leadership terrain. When the band is playing, who does not want to hit the dance floor and lose themselves in the music? Doing so causes us to feel connected with the community, fills us with joy, and transports us from our troubles. That said, from the dance floor, we lack perspective on the whole. Occasionally, we dancers must pull away from the pleasing sense of abandon we have on the dance floor, take a break, and ascend to the balcony to catch our breath. From there, we can see the whole and take in reality from an objective point of view before descending back onto the floor with friends for celebration. Heifetz uses this metaphor to describe the movement of leadership: on the dance floor, we are utterly connected with the community, and on the balcony, we have necessary perspective. The flow between the two is essential for thoughtful leadership.

Technical versus adaptive change. Perhaps Heifetz's best known leadership theoretical framework is the distinction he makes between technical changes, where something needs to be fixed, and adaptive challenges, where a deeper shift must take place. The best way I have found to describe the ways in which technical and adaptive leadership blend together has been the example of the community organization that is considering becoming wheelchair accessible. To add an elevator to a building, widen doors, and build ramps are all technical challenges. But the cognitive shift necessary for an organization to really begin to see how important—how ethically necessary—accessibility is? That is an adaptive challenge. The board meeting where decisions will be made about dedicating resources to accessibility might include a comment like this: "Why do we need to be wheelchair friendly? We don't have any members in wheelchairs." Well, of course we don't; people in wheelchairs cannot get here. In short, technical challenges are ones where the leader needs to change the situation. Adaptive ones require leaders themselves to change.

New incrementalism. I learned of Heifetz's more recent attention to and appreciation for incremental change in a lecture he gave around ten years ago at the school I serve. He spoke in that setting about his growing interest in scientific metaphors for communal leadership and, in that lecture, he focused on DNA. He said that scientists can change, say, 0.1% of a creature's DNA and alter its essential nature, but to change 10% of its DNA would make it incapable of supporting life. Whereas his work on technical versus adaptive change told generations of leaders that tweaking was not enough, Heifetz's attention to science caused him to develop a new appreciation for the dramatic, catalytic effects of incremental change.

I am not the only person who found Heifetz's work life changing. Sharon Daloz Parks is a scholar who has dedicated herself to the study of faith development, especially in young adulthood. During her years at Harvard University, she conducted research on and with Heifetz, and one of the results was her book about Heifetz's teaching methodology, *Leadership Can Be Taught: A Bold Approach for a Complex World.*[5] In her previous work on campus religious life, Daloz Parks used the terms "faith" and "meaning-making" interchangeably. In *Leadership Can Be Taught*, she connects meaning-making with leadership development, and she does so by studying Heifetz's particular way of helping students to develop the cognitive capacity to lead, even in quickly changing situations.

Whereas, in my nearly twenty-five years of appreciating Heifetz, I have focused on his theory of leadership, Daloz Parks focused on his pedagogy. His classes at Harvard's Kennedy School of Government were at times frustrating for students, in that students had to do the heavy lifting of constructing ideas about leadership based on readings and lived experience, including the experience of the classroom dynamic. They wanted "easy answers," as Heifetz's magnum opus' title hints we all do. When observing Heifetz's teaching, Daloz Parks engages with how he equipped students for leadership. Daloz Parks provides a definition of leadership that emerges from Heifetz's teaching: a leader guides a community from dissatisfactory equilibrium, through disequilibrium, to a more satisfying equilibrium.

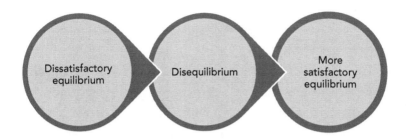

Figure 2: Daloz Parks's interpretation of Heifetz on leadership.

In his teaching, Daloz Parks argues, Heifetz took students on a journey from tacit yet insufficient assumptions about leadership, through disruption and disillusionment, to a more formed understanding of leadership. For many years I adopted this definition of leadership as my own. Only recently has it become apparent to me that it, or any other theory of leadership that relies on "progress"—a linear forward trajectory—no longer serves us well, if indeed it ever did.

What are the shortcomings of Heifetz's definition of leadership, at least in Daloz Parks's interpretation of it? Built into the definition is an assumed telos, an ultimate direction. The definition envisions a plumb line between where we are now and where we want to be, if only we could find that line and grab hold of it. I am starting to think, in these chaotic days, that the line was never there to begin with. Evolutionary biologists in the nineteenth and twentieth centuries argued over the question: is evolution about *improvement*, or merely about adaptation? Ultimately, *adaptation* proved to be what change was all about, and that flummoxed those who believed in a strategic God.

In a similar vein, I do not argue that there is *no* order to the way a community moves toward that which is new; rather I am converting to a new view of what that movement is all about. I used to believe in what a scientist might call an orthogenetic theory of progress, where change happens not sporadically, but according to an innate sense of direction toward the better. I am starting to believe differently, which means my own understanding of leadership and change is evolving as well.

One could make the argument that the three phases Daloz Parks names—dissatisfactory equilibrium, disequilibrium, more satisfactory equilibrium—are simply spread out over so much time that one leader cannot hope to help the community see the Promised Land. We might be finding ourselves today in the midst of a long disequilibrium, where the old ways no longer serve, and a new stability might be so far in the future that we have to find ways to live in the disequilibrium indefinitely. Not unlike the Israelites who thought they would head directly for the Promised Land, but then wandered for more than a generation; and not unlike the Disciples, who thought Jesus would be back within their lifetimes in the form of a second coming—we have to live while we wait.

I think it more likely, however, that Heifetz's definition of leadership (as distilled by Daloz Parks) falls short because there exists no direct through line from dissatisfaction to satisfaction along which the leader can navigate. Optimistic human beings dislike the notion that chaos reigns. I argue that adaptation is anything but chaos, but "progress" might not be the best motivator. Constantly being oriented towards the future can exhaust us when our imaginary depictions of what the future holds are constantly changing. Consider how many organizations have planned, and then replaced plans, and then canceled plans during the pandemic. While institutions burned energy on plans that came to naught, individuals served by those institutions suffered extreme loneliness and disillusionment in their present moments. While progress looks towards the next thing, adaptation is in the present, which is all any of us can know.

I spent my adolescence and young adulthood always focused on the next thing. The results of that focus were mostly satisfying, because times were relatively predictable as compared with today. I applied to only three colleges; my daughter is applying to twenty. I generally found that hard work yielded good results. And still, moving from a future-orientation to a now-orientation was necessary for me to find happiness in my life, and I still work on doing so every day. The communities we serve have only today, and they cannot subsist on a diet of promises for a future equilibrium. Disequilibrium will be with us indefinitely, and in it, we need to adapt in order that we might retain integrity that will hold together not for a short period of churn, but for a churning version of normalcy.

NOTES

4. Ronald A. Heifetz, *Leadership without Easy Answers* (Cambridge, MA: Belknap Press of Harvard University Press, 1994).

5. Sharon Daloz Parks, *Leadership Can Be Taught: A Bold Approach for a Complex World* (Boston: Harvard Business School Press, 2005).

2

THE ORIGINS OF FORWARD-FOCUSED LEADERSHIP THEORIES

The in-between time in which we find ourselves is not a void. It offers opportunities to build incredible lives, meaningful communities, and movements for change. Today's leadership terrain is also not a complete mystery to those who study culture and community. We know something, for example, about the era in which we find ourselves. Scholars of intellectual history in the United States, Canada, and Europe use the defining terms "modern" and "postmodern" to define the changes in how community and leadership have evolved, beginning in the mid-nineteenth century and through the early twenty-first. Some scholars today describe our moment as the advent of a new form of "tribalism," where gathering in communities is happening anew in unexpected ways that are rendered even less predictable by technology.

Just knowing that our eras can be described, if not defined, makes us mindful that, while linearity and progress are not the defining shape for our future, shapelessness and chaos are not the best descriptors either. Buckle up now for a high-speed train ride through three different eras to which I will refer throughout this book. Entire courses of study are designed around each of these eras, so the traveler on this train should keep expectations low as relates to comprehensiveness.

The years between the early to mid-nineteenth century and the 1950s in North America and Europe are known as the modern era. "Humanism" emerged as a dominant anthropology, as many thinkers of the time had faith and hope in virtually limitless human achievements. And why would they not? Technology advanced rapidly during the Industrial Revolution, and a person who believed that culture moved forward in a continuous line toward improvement would understandably expect that, eventually, there would be nothing human beings could not do.

Of course, humanism was problematic even in its heyday. Many of the celebrated technological advances of the era had the express purpose of killing people on a large scale during sometimes avoidable wars. Yet technology and human potential were but two of the dimensions that characterized the modern era. It was also a time period of joining, rule-following, and increasing faith in institutions, including institutions of faith.

During the modern era, institutions flourished in general, and that heyday found its apex in the 1950s. Optimism following the Second World War, reflected in a baby boom, a single-family home building boom, and an influx of students into universities on the GI Bill, shined light on churches. People felt cultural pressure to be in church on Sunday mornings—the only question was where. Mainline Protestantism found itself at the top of the totem pole, although America elected a Roman Catholic president in John F. Kennedy. Notice how these "boom times" left out many people? What about those who were not Christian, or had jobs working in the homes and factories of those Protestant families? Those with less influence lived in the shadows of this sunny time in America.

Rampant joining might have seemed great for the church, but just under the surface, there was... not much under the surface. People often attended religious services as an act of civic duty, not piety; the connection between attendance and belief became thin. Communal life was vibrant, although it was also segregated, class-divided, and oppressive to the majority who had no control over it. The corridors of power—in the academy, politics, and all the technologies whose advancement seemed limitless—were controlled by straight men of European descent and the occasional other who was willing to adopt the behaviors of whiteness and suffer the indignities of bigotry. Those who did not occupy those roles were by-and-large rule-followers, as rules were trusted, even when those rules told people they could not do what they wanted or even what was clearly in their best interest.

The social structures that served as the tent poles of the modern era began to give way in the 1960s. The technologies that seemed destined for limitless progress hit their limits. For example, no scientist could define for humanity when life began—at conception? at the first breath?—so the courts intervened in ways that set rules rather than giving women access to what little agency they had over their bodies. As the true meaning of the atrocities resulting from the use of nuclear warheads at the end of the Second World War sank in, and the Cold War between the US and the USSR struck terror into the hearts of citizens in both nations, the vain hope that weapons could end all wars—if only the ultimate weapon could warn challengers away—crumbled in leaders' hands.

The 1960s were years marred by the assassinations of leaders who inspired hope, disrupted by the questioning of every type of authority, and liberated by a society-wide awakening to the injustice of cultural control in the hands of an elite and questionably qualified few. In this, they marked the passage from the modern to the postmodern eras. Postmodernity is best described as a time when certain societal rules were exposed in their arbitrariness. Freedoms rose, but along with those freedoms came the undermining of the institutions that held the society together, for better and for worse. If the clock could be turned back, what might have been a better result of the societal disruptions of the 1960s would have been the emergence of principles over principalities: instead of investing our confidence in a class or a set of institutions, humanity might have come together around a set of shared values, such as love for the earth, or an ethic of mutual respect among human beings. Instead, rules were thrown out, like babies with bathwater.

The postmodern era witnessed the crumbling of monolithic Truth (singular, with a capital T) and their replacement by multiple truths (plural, with a lower-case t) vying for their seats at the table. The results for so many—including women like me—were life-giving. All three of the schools I attended for secondary and post-secondary education had been all-male less than a generation before I had the opportunity to learn in them. I was ordained in a tradition that had long welcomed women into the pulpit, but mine was the first generation of women who had predecessors on whose shoulders we could stand. For institutions, the authority-questioning of the postmodern era was a helpful corrective, but that questioning sometimes overcorrected.

Society still needed what social critic William May calls "intermediate institutions."[6] Churches and civic organizations fall into that category. Between the family and the populace as a whole, intermediate institutions provide services and centers for belonging. Their strength during the modern era took pressure off families and the body politic, and their weakening placed pressure on those two entities that they were not prepared to withstand. As I write this chapter, a presidential election is unfolding, and the Senate is preparing to ram through the nomination of a Supreme Court justice with little time with which to handle the process thoughtfully and well. When I step back from the chaos about which I read in the news, it occurs to me that the president and the Supreme Court simply should not have this much power over our society and my life. But the systematic weakening of every entity that stands between me and them creates an overreliance on those at the very top. Like pulled taffy, the weak center gives way.

In their epic tome on religion in the United States today, *American Grace: How Religion Divides and Unites Us*,[7] Robert Putnam and David Campbell describe the disruptive events of the 1960s as a "shock," followed by two "aftershocks." The shock of the 1960s struck at the moral foundation of the United States, especially around sexual mores, calling into question anything one might describe as normative rules. The earthquake exposed the weak foundation—the arbitrariness—of modernity's so-called rules. Why should white men run the world and everyone else live with what they decide? Why should people be separated by race, and can separate ever be equal? Why should women serve as indentured servants to their husbands, caring for home and children with no opportunities to have or pursue their own dreams? Every question created a vibration, and those vibrations intensified into an earthquake: a ten on the Richter scale. The two aftershocks shaped the postmodern era to come, especially as related to religion. Before describing the two aftershocks, it is important to point out religion's variety and diversity in the United States. Sociologists like Putnam and his coauthors tend to generalize about certain religious groups, and they have data to back up those generalizations, but none dares paint all religion with a broad brush. That said, the patterns *American Grace* describes require the conflation of important differences among groups. With that caveat in mind, I proceed in presenting *American Grace*'s framework, borrowing their categories with all humility, especially as relates to internal diversity within groups.

The first aftershock to the earthquake that was the long sixties, according to Putnam and Campbell, came in the form of the rise of the Religious Right. Conservative Christians were in some cases appalled by morality's crumbling. Others saw that disintegration as a tremendous opportunity to carve out space for religious conservatives in the corridors of power in Washington and on Wall Street. They pointed to the free-wheeling morality of the 1960s, and to the social costs associated with the loss of shared rules of conduct, and told America that they had a good alternative.

The Religious Right presented an even more rigid set of social codes than modernity's norms and welcomed aboard those overwhelmed by the pace and chaos of change that the 1960s presented. Those social codes applied to sexuality in particular, which should tip us off as to their less-than-Biblical motivations. The Religious Right took little interest in poverty and class issues arterial to the Gospel, and they embraced imperial political motivations that the prophets and Jesus decried. They were deeply concerned, however, about traditional gender roles and, later, sexual orientation. The Bible gives little attention to sexuality compared with its concern, especially Jesus', for the poor. Sex is bad; greed is fine? The Religious Right was not, in fact, motivated by religion, but by gaining access to power by consolidating the energies of those shaken by rapid change.

Consider this example, found in Glennon Doyle's *Untamed*:[8] religious conservatives drawn to the Religious Right come in large part from Evangelical Christian churches more so than from the politically mixed Roman Catholic or Orthodox traditions. Evangelical theology, until the 1960s, led scholars to believe that human life starts with the first breath. Seeing an opportunity to mobilize political interests and influence, religious leaders altered that stance to suggest that life begins with conception.

For two to three generations since, religious conservatives have staunchly opposed abortion, in most cases not realizing that the position they are taking relates more to a decision on the part of political operatives than to a theological belief evangelicals have "always" held. This example is not meant to suggest that those who oppose abortion are foolish, or that abortion rights are self-evident. Rather, the shift of position on abortion on the part of evangelicals, spurred by the political motivations of the Religious Right, give us perspective on how backlash against the changing morality of the 1960s had both political and religious dimensions.

Those who saw the way in which some used religion to resist social change became disillusioned with religion itself, seeing how easily it had been coopted and distorted. Putnam and Campbell refer to that disillusionment with religion, and a related exodus from the pews, as the second aftershock to follow the earthquake that was the 1960s.

As the disillusionment of the 1960s cultural revolutions broke apart the façade of a monolithic white, Protestant America, American Christianity's complicity with oppression became more and more apparent, and the hypocrisy embedded in that complicity became impossible to ignore. Religion had made a deal. I will not go so far as to say it made a deal with the devil, but I think it fair to say it made a deal with modernity: "Include us in your institution boom, modernity, and we won't ask too many questions about who is getting forgotten and pressed down." The deal backfired. Mainline Christianity's cooperation with secular society's season of institutional influence meant that, as the institution boom waned, the mainline lost influence.

Mainline Christianity did participate, so to speak, in the 1960s. The Black Christian Church played a significant role in the Civil Rights Movement and resistance to the Vietnam War. William Sloane Coffin preached mightily against the forces of empire from the pulpit of Battell Chapel at Yale University, a bastion of cultural influence in the mainline. Furthermore, mainline Christian thinkers were aware and critical of the ways in which Christianity was changing with culture. Harvey Cox wrote *The Secular City: Secularization and Urbanization in Theological Perspective*[9] about the ways in which culture was changing, and how the church needed to change with it. Like conservative voices in many movements, however, the Religious Right was much louder than the mainline and offered pithier slogans. The mainline failed to present a compelling counternarrative to it, and the two very different ways of being Christian found themselves lumped together in the black-and-white American mind. As much as I wish otherwise, since the early nineteenth century, the church has not been as much a social justice leader as follower,[10] partly because culture shapes religion more quickly than religion can catch up to shape culture.

Because of the energy generated by the first aftershock—the rise of the Religious Right—Evangelical churches were energized in the early postmodern era. Not so the mainline. Therefore, the disillusionment of the second aftershock—disillusionment with religion—ironically struck hardest at the segment of the Christian community that was—unlike the Evangelical churches that were resisting social change—more open to repentance. Mainline Christians, over the course of one or two generations, exited the church en masse. This departure was a matter of guilt by association. Being Christian in America was suddenly laden with unappealing, heavy baggage.

The way in which the mainline had cooperated with modernity became its downfall. It modeled itself on other institutions, and they were becoming weaker too. That modeling included values of free association and voluntary participation, so barriers to departure were low. The mainline found itself cold in the shadow cast by the more judgmental, exclusive, and oppressive dimensions of the Religious Right, and with no cultural pressure to stick with church, mainline Christians departed.

Today, the fastest-growing demographic category in American religion is the "nones." In fact, any other group that seems to be growing is likely doing so due to immigration and birthrates within those traditions, not attraction of newcomers to their ways. Nones—more specifically described as "spiritual but religiously unaffiliated"—are not to be confused with atheists, or even agnostics. It is a group that claims no membership but might or might not have an inclination toward faith and community.

The postmodern era was a time when membership in anything became less appealing. In a different and earlier book, *Bowling Alone: The Collapse and Revival of American Community*,[11] Robert Putnam wrote extensively about the deterioration of "social capital" in the United States. He argued that decline in a shared value for joining and participating in intermediate associations beyond the family led to the fraying of society. *Bowling Alone* came out twenty years ago, and since then, a newly tribal era has begun to emerge in which associations—often fostered by technology—are on the rise again in unpredictable ways. Yet membership in religious organizations seems to be continuing to move in the other direction, away from cohesion and toward a desire on the part of many to keep their options open.

In *American Grace*, Putnam and Campbell offer extensive analysis of what causes a person to stick with the religion of their childhood or find a new one in adulthood. Patterns suggest that religious tendencies transfer strongly within families; three-fourths of those surveyed claim the religion of their childhoods as their own. Similarly, those raised with no religious affiliation tend to remain nones. Politics have a strong influence as well. Evangelicals who are politically liberal tend to move toward the mainline, whereas evangelical conservatives stay put in evangelicalism. Catholics tend to have an almost ethnic sense of affiliation with their tradition; non-observant Catholics are likely to describe themselves as Catholic nonetheless, whereas there really is no such thing as a non-practicing mainline Christian in the American religious lexicon. Many mainline denominations, including my own United Church of Christ, are attempting to rebrand themselves as politically liberal alternatives within the Christian context, while two generations ago they were so dominant they did not need to be alternatives to anything. Putnam and Campbell argue that such rebranding does not happen overnight.[12]

Neither, however, does secularization. Putnam and Campbell take great pains to present the difference between generational and life-cycle change in religious practice. These terms drawn from sociology suggest that we must compare people of the same age in different generations to detect patterns of secularization. Most people become more religious as they get older. Compare one person when they were twenty-five as opposed to fifty-five, and you cannot make grand claims about what is happening in a culture. Compare a twenty-five-year-old from 1940 with one from 1980 or 2020 and you can see patterns of secularization emerge.

According to Putnam and Campbell, even taking the nones into account, American society is indeed becoming more secular, but far more gradually than one might think by looking at mainline Christian church attendance patterns, and far less significantly than the verifiably secular Western Europe. Put differently, the United States is and remains a very religious country, and statistically, a very Christian one. The rise of the nones deteriorated mainline Christianity's sense of cultural centrality. Never having had to defend itself ideologically in the US previously, the mainline went from cultural powerhouse to embattlement on every side: most notably, the secular left and the religious right. The mainline never quite figured out how to define itself over and against the Puritanical backlash against the cultural transformation of the 1960s; all religious persons were branded as prudes. The mainline similarly never presented an argument for religious practice as a better alternative to secularism in a society where joining in and of itself was not a desirable practice.

To say that the mainline never figured itself out amidst post-modernism would be bad news were it not for the fact that the postmodern era is ending. In this newly tribal time, desire for belonging and joining is reasserting itself. Although it was never fully defined—never even really had its own name except to say it was "post-" what came before it—the postmodern era is giving way, and religious leaders would be wise to gather as many learnings as possible and then focus on the future.

People are gathering again; today, they do so even amidst a pandemic, against the rules. Perhaps they never stopped, but when it comes to ideological sameness, togetherness is intensifying. Gathering looks different, surely, due to technology, but just as importantly, gatherings are tending to be even more homogenous than in the past. Social groupings take place in new settings—such as cohorts that know each other only on the internet—and individuals hold many different affiliations at once. My deep hope is that this societal season of people finding one another in pockets gives us a new opportunity to right the wrong of the overcorrection of the postmodern era. What if we, in this time of new tribalism, gather around principles that give new life, instead of rallying around the already powerful (like that which characterized modernity) or rallying around nothing at all (post-modernity)?

Principles transcend individuals and even transcend time and space. Principles are more specific than philosophies and less restrictive than politics. I fear that a principles-based mode will not become the dominant mode of communal leadership anytime soon. It seems many who supported former president Donald Trump did so despite understanding him to be a fundamentally selfish, attention-obsessed, even violent person (towards women, which his adherents seem to find acceptable). A new era of principled leadership might not take root during our lifetimes. Between now and then, how, exactly, are we supposed to lead and be led?

NOTES

6. William F. May, *Beleaguered Rulers: The Public Obligation of the Professional*, 1st ed. (Louisville, KY: Westminster John Knox Press, 2001).

7. Robert D. Putnam and David Campbell, *American Grace: How Religion Divides and Unites Us* (New York: Simon & Schuster, 2010).

8. Glennon Doyle, *Untamed* (New York: The Dial Press, 2020).

9. Harvey Cox, *The Secular City: Secularization and Urbanization in Theological Perspective* (Princeton, NJ: Princeton University Press, 2013). First edition published in 1965.

10. Putnam and Campbell, *American Grace*, 315.

11. Robert D. Putnam, *Bowling Alone: The Collapse and Revival of American Community* (New York: Simon & Schuster, 2000).

12. Putnam and Campbell, *American Grace*, 131.

3

AVAILABLE ALTERNATIVES TO FORWARD-FOCUSED LEADERSHIP THEORIES

To suggest that all leadership theory has a future-leaning bent to it would be untrue, even arrogant. Let us briefly explore some other leadership theories currently in use so as to situate intentional leadership on a wider landscape of theories. Few leaders devote enough attention to the theory they use to guide their work, which is unfortunate given how much harder leadership is without mental models serving as guides. Therefore, situating intentional leadership serves the double purpose of describing a new theory while also offering up other options to readers.

COMMUNITY ORGANIZING

Whereas intentional leadership is all about managing and maintaining the ironic juxtapositions of human engagement, community organizing is all about dialogue. The role of the community organizer is to foster dialogue among those suffering under systemic oppression and helping them to name and question their circumstances. As I write in *Dynamic Discernment: Reason, Emotion, and Power in Change Leadership*,[13] power sustains itself by hiding in plain sight. Those who suffer under unfair uses of power do not necessarily see that they have their own power because, by comparison with those keeping them from advancement, they feel they do not. Community organizers create settings where, through dialogue, those who are oppressed come to recognize their shared experiences and the power in their numbers. Whereas oppressors are expert at turning the subjugated against one another, convincing them that they are different from one another, dialogue shows people how much they have in common, including their common enemies.

When blending concepts from community organizing and liberation theology, we find that dialogue as a primary tool of leadership enables catharsis for oppressors, too, for each of us are oppressors in some parts of our lives. I think, for example, about how much I have been ordering online during the pandemic. The Instacart delivery persons who bring us our groceries are people I have never met before, and yet I ask them to do something for me that I do not wish to do out of anxiety about Covid-19 and lack of time due to my own job. I am not in dialogue with that person to know their sorrows and what I might be doing to alleviate them. Tempting as it is to say I can relate to community organizers, and the oppressed they bring together, I have a hand in every role in the drama of oppression, including the role of "oppressor."

Liberation theologian Paolo Freire wrote that the ultimate goal of the liberator is consciousness.[14] Through dialogue, the oppressor and the oppressed become conscious of the fact that they are playing out roles, reading lines from a script in a play they did not realize they were staging. Becoming conscious is the beginning of liberation, but the trick is that the oppressor and the oppressed both must become conscious of the invisible forces that are moving them about on earth and begin to pull back on them. Otherwise, the oppressed are likely to overthrow the oppressor but then become just like them, perpetuating a cycle, and setting the scene for the new oppressors to be overthrown next, without ever becoming conscious of the stage on which they are acting.

LARGE-GROUP DYNAMICS

Yet another theoretical framework for engaging leadership comes to us from Peter Block, consultant and writer on large-group dynamics, in his book *Community: The Structure of Belonging*.[15] I read the book with a sense of wonder and discovery. For so much of my working life, I have experienced the assumption on the part of those I have led that I know something about how to build community. Over time, I have learned, but in the early years, I faked it. Now, as an educator for aspiring ministers, I am much more conscious—intentional—about the necessity of teaching them how to build community. The main pedagogical tool I use for teaching community building is reflective practice: we build community, and then we talk about how we did it and what our decisions meant. Still, theory helps, and Block's has had a significant impact on me.

Block argues that what brings people together is consideration of possibilities over problems. No more taking for granted, he tells us, that we know how to come together. We need rules and tools, and privileging possibilities over problems is one helpful rule. We need to consciously emphasize the positive and the future, not the complaints and the past; we must use every opportunity to be together to model how we ought to be in community with each other. In Block's model, the main role of the leader is to convene the community and structure belonging among all. Delegating is not part of his system, in that the leader never hoarded power and control to begin with. Block writes that obsession with problems and overdependence on leaders are signs of institutional unhealth.

Block tells us to focus on our power to bring about change and the positive possibilities change might bring. One might call Block's leadership theory a macro-, institution-level version of the habits of heart that emerge from the leadership practice of Appreciative Inquiry.[16] Appreciative Inquiry, which emerged from the business world, provides a guide for engagement between individuals that draws out positive possibilities. A conversation or interview guided by the technique will include the questioner asking about what gives the answerer hope and joy. The questioner asks for abundant illustrations and examples, as telling stories ignites creativity and inspiration. Those who study Appreciative Inquiry and its results find that the emphasis on the positive and the possible changes the shape of interactions and the people engaging in those interactions, down to the level of their neurological responses.

With his focus on large-group dynamics, Block's *Structure of Belonging* sets the stage for community building that promotes optimism and creativity over complaints and problem solving. One could blend Block's admonition that we focus on possibilities over problems with Appreciative Inquiry as the leader moves in and out of group settings, versus one-on-one engagements. Whereas Appreciative Inquiry provides a method for members of the community engaging each other, Block argues that leaders can build the way we gather in such a way that appreciation emerges from each participant in the community.

Community organizing, and group dynamics shaped by engaging possibilities over problems, each provide frameworks that guide leaders in real time. A community-organizing mindset will cause a leader to promote dialogue and consciousness. The leader with a possibilities mindset will seek to reframe issues in favor of options, alternatives, and possible directions. How does "intentional leadership," the new theoretical framework described in this book, function as a guiding principle? What would be the habits of mind of the intentional leader? How would intentional leadership guide their actions within their roles?

NOTES

13. Sarah B. Drummond, *Dynamic Discernment: Reason, Emotion, and Power in Change Leadership* (Cleveland: The Pilgrim Press, 2019).

14. Paulo Freire, *Pedagogy of the Oppressed* (New York: Bloomsbury, 2014).

15. Peter Block, *Community: The Structure of Belonging* (San Francisco: Berrett-Koehler Publishers, 2008).

16. David Cooperrider and Ron Fry of the Weatherhead School at Case Western Reserve University developed the concept of Appreciative Inquiry in the late 1980s.

4

A TIME FOR NEW
THEORIES TO EMERGE

So far, I have laid out a conundrum. Institutions built around a combination of habit and undeserved power have proven themselves unworthy of the task of holding community together. A leadership era built around shared and lofty principles rather than demagogues or bylaws—that new Promised Land—is not yet ready to emerge. Distrust of institutions has proven destructive, especially when it results from setting aside facts and truth, yet we cannot return to an era of institutions managing all human togetherness. Our society has become extremely complex, yet we have to move forward. Thus, I have painted a picture of an in-between time, and in an in-between time, those who carry communal responsibility need to do their duty.

What is the nature of that duty? Even that question is under reconsideration today. I write in *Sharing Leadership: A United Church of Christ Way of Being in Community* about how leadership works amidst flat hierarchies. When stakeholders in communities do not have a shared understanding of the leader's responsibility, the community will likely default to a top-down structure, at least in its expectations. Yet few organizations function best when leadership is consolidated by few from on-high. Today, the leader's duty usually requires bringing the community closer together while orienting it toward a more life-giving way. A new leadership theory can help leaders function in that role more effectively while also resetting communal expectations for what leaders are supposed to do.

However insufficient, however incomplete, leaders today need models, or what social scientists call "theoretical frameworks." Amidst complicated times, our brains seek shortcuts that make it possible to quickly process a great deal of information, much of it new and unfamiliar. Cognitive scientists call these shortcuts "schemata," which is the plural form of the word "schemes." Schemata help us to identify danger, which is perhaps why they are so difficult to dislodge once they have taken hold. We see a car with blue lights in our rearview mirror, making a howling sound, and we pull over before we start processing what has happened. The gift of leadership theory is that we can build our own schemata for leadership situations that hone our instincts and prepare us to process. Then, those schemata can become habit.

Here is an example of a leadership theory that has become habit for me: when working with a person who is extremely upset, I check myself and monitor my own emotions rather than going along with them on the reactive ride. I know from leadership theory (specifically, emotional systems theory and books like Rabbi Edwin Friedman's *A Failure of Nerve*[17]) that the leader who remains the self-differentiated picture of equanimity is more capable of effectiveness amidst emotional intensity. I know that there was a time early in my working life when I engaged upset with more upset. I can remember an argument in a teacher's lounge in a college summer school teaching job, where I and another teacher had a yelling match so intense that another teacher intervened, but I do not recognize the version of me that became so worked up and made a bad situation much worse.

Here is an example of a new leadership theory I created recently, on-the-fly. My spouse is a high school teacher, and both he and I had to prepare this past summer for a school year like none we had ever known. We were preparing to teach amidst pandemic protocols and did not know what to expect. Not only did we have to follow health safety guidelines that were new, we also were to be working with uncertain and anxious people who had not seen each other in-person in six months. I made a comment amidst a conversation about what such uncertainty called for, and Dan—an English teacher, excellent with words—refined it, and it became a household leadership theory: "When a community knows where it's going, leaders make plans. When a community doesn't, or can't, leaders make space. Something new needs to happen in that space."

A leadership theory distills patterns from human interactions in communal settings that have implications for the motivation and guidance of those communities. Whereas the study of organizational behavior describes patterns, leadership theory moves into the implications of those patterns for those called forth to bring communities closer to their shared goals and vision. For example, an observation from someone concerned with organizational behavior might be that even the best ideas for institutions or societies have some opponents and resisters. Someone concerned with leadership theory would go a step further to state that it is important for leaders to listen to resisters but also to move past the resistance of unhealthy people who instinctively dig in against even the most life-giving change. Therefore, a leadership theory includes both an observation and an implication for practice that can be deployed, by the experienced leader, out of sheer muscle memory in the heat of the moment.

Scholarly research on leadership falls into two broad categories: quantitative methods that rely on numbers, and qualitative methods that analyze words. The differences between the two approaches are far vaster than numbers and words, however. A quantitative researcher posits a hypothesis and uses numbers to prove it as a theory. A qualitative researcher seeks to create a thick description of a lived experience, valid (accurate) and reliable (predictive of a wider pattern). A qualitative researcher does not present a hypothesis, nor does the qualitative researcher prove anything. Their success is found in the form of deep and new understanding.

In a similar way, leadership theory is useful insofar as it makes sense of that which might otherwise seem random. Theories provide standards of excellence for leaders and the possibility of ongoing improvement and growth. Leadership theory closes the gap between experienced leaders, who create patterns—or schemata— over time, on the job, and novice leaders who have not had time to gather such lessons but are willing to study to take up their responsibilities. Leadership theory provides guidance in uncharted waters, and writing as I am in the year 2020, all waters seem to be those previously unnavigated. Finally, and perhaps most importantly for me, as I consider writing and teaching about leadership as a ministry, leadership theory helps leaders feel less crazy. Organizational behavior, as helpful and useful as it is, simply describes the ways in which communities can sabotage themselves and choose death-dealing ways. Leadership theory provides the possibility that, with an understanding of human behavior patterns, leaders need not fly blind.

The study of leadership theory is a relatively new, multidisciplinary area of inquiry. Before it emerged, those who studied leadership were most often historians who embraced what we now call the "Great Man" theory of leadership.[18] That theory, now roundly dismissed, suggested that leadership was all about the leader—the choices he (and it was almost always "he") made and the bravery he exhibited—and his greatness or flaws.

Certainly, biographers still write about great human beings who accomplished much. At the same time, scholars of all stripes have come to understand that the greatness of a leader has much to do with the situations in which leaders find themselves. The interaction of their gifts—and even their flaws—with the times have a lot more to do with their success than was once thought. A study on Franklin D. Roosevelt and Winston Churchill today is more likely to assess their achievements under consideration of the surroundings that made their specific attributes what was needed at the time, rather than point to their decisions as independently heroic, *sui generis* causes.

Leadership theories today are more systematic and consider the way in which the leader can influence complex dynamics, while also cooperating with those dynamics. Two examples of bodies of theory that take complexity into account without seeking to oversimplify are "emotional systems theory" and "emergence." Emotional systems theory, originally the terrain of psychologists who study and work with families, suggests that people in a community are emotionally intertwined. Much like the root systems of trees connect with each other deep underground, the emotional structures on which we are built affect each other in profound ways. A therapist who believes deeply in emotional systems might treat a particular patient but would view the entire family surrounding that patient as the real client, with the one seeking treatment serving as symptom-bearer for the whole system's affliction.

Theories of emergence are like emotional systems theory in that they attend to what one might call naturally occurring phenomena. Emergence theory suggests that solutions to complex problems are not created by people but rather gestate in healthy communities and are born in their own time. The leader's role in such cases is to create that healthy setting for new ideas to take shape and become viable.

Out of all the definitions of emergence I have read over the years, my favorite comes from a parable from Susan Beaumont's book on liminal leadership.[19] She writes of a fictional church clean-up day, where a group of volunteers arrives with a mandate but no clear plan or instructions. After a bit of trial and error as the group negotiates an approach, with some awkwardness and perhaps even a hurt feeling or two, a plan emerges. Decisions unfold whereby different volunteers match up with tasks that suit their abilities and interests. The wise leader does not try to control emergence but rather encourages the natural distribution of tasks and gifts while getting out of the way. Emergence theory suggests that what rises up out of chaos is authentic, self-perpetuating, and thus more likely to succeed than any top-down, imposed structure. The challenge for leadership is making space, helping people to stay calm within that space, and not rushing to closure before a new way is ready to be born.

My interest in the study of leadership could be characterized as a passion that emerged; emergency being a more accurate metaphor than that of a vision or a journey. I became interested in leadership theory for the same reason I love long conversations with thoughtful people: as expressed earlier, I am a meaning-of-life enthusiast. Making sense of patterns of human interactions is a source of great satisfaction for me. When I was a child, I—like most, surely—asked "why" about all I saw. As a teen, I was drawn to friends who liked to deconstruct the motivations of others, sometimes getting myself in trouble for gossiping; surely my motivations were as often puerile as pure. In college, I dedicated serious time to thinking and talking about the meaning of the friendships I was choosing and forming, and choices related to an academic major and extracurricular foci. I was privileged to have a financially supportive family who made it possible for me to consider such decisions in light of their self-actualization potential and inherent virtue, rather than as means to a necessary end. I never took that privilege for granted, although I am sure my parents worried more than once about how I expected to make a living from deep conversations (mission accomplished).

Only after significant higher education and work experience in campus administration and ministry did I come to know that my passion for questions regarding what to do with one's life had a scholarly implication: discernment, vocation, and career theory. During doctoral coursework and research on educational leadership, I became curious and then passionate about how leaders could create programs that would provide structure and guidance to people who want to make deeper sense of their lives like I did. The research question I formulated as I prepared to write a dissertation on the topic was this: "How do religious leaders move from a theological concept to a program, without ruining the concept or creating a program that could never work?" That question has never let me down, in that I still have not come close to answering it and never expect to in any final way.

Program planning and evaluation is a small subfield in the study of educational administration. It was the name of the first course I took and the first course I later taught. One of the most important tools in the field is the theoretical framework. Those frameworks help to describe a pattern of interactions between human influence and human behavior. Sometimes, they come in the form of words; other times, diagrams. This semester I am teaching in a hybrid model, where some of my students are online and others face-to-face in masks due to pandemic protocols. Students online cannot see the whiteboard if they are online, and my writing and drawing in the whiteboard tool in our online learning platform is messy and awkward. I have been stunned by how much less relaxed and effective I feel when unable to draw diagrams during a leadership class. Diagrammatic theoretical frameworks are part of how I teach and how I think.

Here is an example of a theoretical framework I developed in the midst of a consulting engagement with an institution dedicated to teaching theology and religion, and then included in a wider framework on planning and evaluation in the book, *Holy Clarity: The Practice of Planning and Evaluation*.[20] In education and ministry, we are quick to introduce new programs when problems arise, but we sometimes do not take the time to articulate the answer to this question: what is the problem we are trying to solve? Is this the right solution? Is it even the right problem?

I found myself in a conversation about an interaction at a university among campus religious leaders and a senior administrator. Campus religious leaders had coalesced around the idea that they needed a shared staff person in the form of a director with an office and staff. At the time, like many universities, this campus's religious needs were served in part by a university chaplain and in part by ministers, rabbis, and Islamic chaplains who were primarily accountable to faith communities and denominational structures. The campus ministers in the latter category wanted a new kind of representation and worked hard to land an appointment with a senior administrator to make their case. The meeting began with the religious leaders describing what they wanted, but the university administrator redirected them. "What is the problem you are trying to solve?" The religious leaders again delved into the topic of what they wanted the administrator to do, she asked the question again, and they could not answer it. The meeting was over in less than ten minutes.

Soon after hearing this story, I was engaged in some consulting on evaluation strategies. The think tank I was assisting was having trouble evaluating their programs because those programs had lost touch with the problem they were established to solve. I drew the condition/intervention diagram during a conversation. The circle represents the organization's mission: what is the change it is trying to make for the wider world? The arrow represents the programs the institution carries out. In light of that diagram, it was clear that some arrows were more tangential to the circle, rather than direct hits to the mission in question. I went on to develop this model for the sake of evaluation planning. In light of this new perspective—"what is the problem you are trying to solve?" and the condition/intervention diagram—the purpose of evaluation was to track change in the circle. The effectiveness of programs—those represented by the arrow—could only be assessed with changes to the condition in mind.

I tell the origin story of the condition/intervention diagram as an argument in favor of developing and then using theoretical frameworks as part of our reflective practice on leadership. I had one conversation in one context about a campus religious life issue.

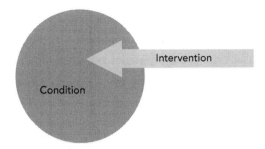

Figure 3: Condition/Intervention Diagram

I brought learning from that context into a different setting, role, and type of organization. Contemplation has its place and necessity, but that which can be carried from one leadership challenge to another is the theoretical framework that emerges from contemplation and analysis. This book introduces an original theoretical framework that I call "Intentional Leadership," along with five sub-frameworks, each meant to provide a structure for leadership and programmatic assessment and evaluation.

The leadership theory presented in this book is somewhat more complex than the condition/intervention diagram, but that is not the most significant difference between the new theory and the one developed previously. The condition/intervention diagram is, like most leadership theories, built on the assumption that the leader's job is to foster progress. In this book, I argue that progress has become such a fraught concept that it no longer deserves to be at the foundation of the guidance that leaders give and receive.

In my book *Dynamic Discernment: Reason, Emotion, and Power in Change Leadership*,[21] I write about perspectives on change leadership from three different schools of thought: the business world (reason), the social sciences attendant to emotional systems (emotion), and liberation theology (power). I attempt in that book to present go-to leadership practices that match onto each of those three perspectives on change, arguing that the leader's job is to discern which dynamic is most influential in a given moment and to choose the approach that matches the dynamic. Even that relatively complex set of arguments, which called for leaders' counterintuitive self-modification in light of circumstances, shows that an assumption of the possibility of progress underlies every dynamic and leadership strategy. This season in human history requires something different and something more than progress as the sole motivator and guide.

Today, leaders find themselves cobbling together numerous partially insufficient theories in order to help them get through day after day of making decisions that affect others and the world. The *stage theories* of leadership prevalent in the business world suggest that leaders guide communities through a series of steps that eventuate in arrival at a shared purpose. Most stage theories begin with casting a vision and setting goals, and end with institutionalizing progress once it is arrived upon. What happens when "arrival" is simply not an option?

Emotional systems theory suggests that leaders can, through their self-differentiation and nonanxiety, help a community land at a place of satisfactory homeostasis, free of triangulation, where no one vulnerable person bears the symptoms of the sick whole. But when homeostasis is in the eye of the beholder, resistant to definition (let alone shared ownership), how does the leader know when anything resembling a destination has been reached? Where is the motivating energy for leaders in managing emotional systems, defusing the bombs planted by unhealthy saboteurs?

Liberation theology suggests that the institution or society will have succeeded when all have become liberated, and the same will have failed when the oppressed simply become new oppressors.

But power is so elusive, quick to hide when a light is shone upon it, and individual leaders can do little to overturn systemic oppression in the short run. How will the leader make day-to-day decisions in the face of such bulwarks against so-called progress? This book suggests a different kind of plumb line than "progress," "healthy systems," or "liberation." Each is a worthy goal, but all three change dynamics explored in *Dynamic Discernment* imagine a telos, or destination point, "out there." They all look to a horizon, which risks the leader focusing on that which they cannot control: namely, everything except themselves. This book suggests that the horizon is within, at a sweet spot between tensions that seek balance not in pulling toward a future goal, but inside us. By setting the goal of inner balance among juxtaposing tensions, the leader reorients the purpose of leadership to an energy within— both within the leader as an individual and within the community served—toward that which can be achieved in an in-between time.

Chapter 5 will delve deeply into the nature of *liminality* in which new tribalism is currently emerging, and the necessity of discernment for leaders in the midst of it.

NOTES

17. Edwin H. Friedman, *A Failure of Nerve: Leadership in the Age of the Quick Fix* (New York: Seabury Books, 2007).

18. Louis W. Fry, "Toward a Theory of Spiritual Leadership," *The Leadership Quarterly* 14, no. 6 (2003): 693–727, 696, doi:10.1016/j.leaqua.2003.09.001.

19. Beaumont, *How to Lead When You Don't Know Where You're Going*.

20. Sarah B. Drummond, *Holy Clarity: The Practice of Planning and Evaluation* (Herndon, VA: Alban Institute, 2009).

21. Drummond, *Dynamic Discernment*.

5

LIMINALITY AND DISCERNMENT

Today is November 4, 2020. I went to bed last night to the sound of newscasters calling out election results like auctioneers, with every sentence—every phrase—dripping with caveats. They made clear that we might not know the results of the presidential race until later, maybe days later, because early voting left many ballots to count with care. When I began to feel like the tension was too much, I went through my ordinary evening routine and went to bed, where my subconscious processed the possibilities through my dreams. When morning came, my spouse and I stayed in bed, where he opened his phone—where it is usually not allowed—and read to me that the race is too close to call. There were only three possible outcomes of last night's election reporting: one candidate won decisively, the other one did, or we still would not know. That option three was the result is not surprising at all in 2020, a year of anxious in-betweenness, as 2020 is a distillation of a broader societal pattern.

In Chapter 2, I provided an overview of sweeping cultural patterns ranging from the modern era to the postmodern era into a newly tribal season. New tribalism provides the opportunity for a new beginning for community life, particularly for religious communities, but faith communities must tangle with the baggage they carried with them from modernity, through postmodernity, and into this new time. Much of that baggage ought to have been left behind an era ago. In the book of Genesis, we read that when God created the earth, the universe was a "formless void" (Gen 1:1). The era in which we find ourselves is formless, but it is not a void. Leadership amidst formlessness requires an understanding of what constitutes community in this space, which might lack definition but is anything but empty.

Consider the common quip one hears from those who do not dedicate much time to thinking about those topics. The quip: "Oh, nobody goes to church anymore." In New England, the relatively secular region of the country where I reside, one sees churches at the center of every town, and a casual observer might deduce that they were once full every Sunday but are now mostly empty but for a few hardy souls. To think that religion is on the wane would be logical. In *American Grace*, Putnam and Campbell tell us, however, that America remains an exceedingly religious nation as compared with its European counterparts.[22] The religions that are growing, however, are not the ones that use the churches on the town greens. They are churches formed by and catering to immigrants, for instance; they are non-Christian; they are Evangelical congregations with strong small-group ministries. The notion that "no one" goes to church anymore results from using the past as a lens and pointing it at the present, which of course will limit how much we see.

When we consider the cultural eras that have defined the past two hundred years in North America and Europe, we see a movement from distinctiveness to nebulousness. The modern era, which included the Industrial Revolution, found definition in humanism, or a shared sense of humanity's nearly limitless potential. It gave way to the postmodern era, which, as mentioned in Chapter One, never even got its own name. It was just post- what had come before. New tribalism is not even a term widely used; if I did not study cultural movements as part of my focus on leadership, I probably would never have picked up on it. All this to say that the North American population has continuously moved away from cultural consensus as to the nature of reality since the 1960s. We are in an in-between time without any sense of whether cohesion will be on the other side of this era; in-betweenness might be the proverbial "new normal." One way to define a stabilized in-betweenness is "liminality."

In her book, *How to Lead When You Don't Know Where You're Going: Leading in a Liminal Season*,[23] Susan Beaumont tells us that the word "liminality" comes from the root, "limen," which means threshold. When we live on a threshold between that which is over, and that which has yet to begin, we could spend our energy on patience and waiting, we could spend it attending to the present moment, or we can spend it preparing for what is to come. We need to do all three, and yet none of those practices—cultivating patience, active attending to the now, or preparation— match conventional expectations for leadership.

Although it is in-between, liminality is not a void. Liminality possesses its own nuanced characteristics worthy of exploration. Beaumont defines a liminal season as one where "watching and waiting can be difficult, overplanning can be futile, and it simply isn't helpful to pretend that we understand what happens next."[24] No one makes a general announcement, like a train conductor, saying, "We are now entering a liminal season." We are usually well into one before it even dawns on us that the previous season is over. Some markers that we are in in-between times include individual frustration that old, familiar management practices simply do not work; unexpected disengagement on the part of members of the community; and a growing, shared sense that normalcy as we once knew it will never return and is perhaps not worthy of our striving or grit.

The Covid-19 pandemic provides an eerily perfect example of the nature of liminality. As I write this chapter, there is no sign of when it will be over. Many workers have lost their jobs and are unsure whether those jobs, or even their associated industries, will recover. I, for one, have taken up new leadership practices I am unlikely to let go after the pandemic is over. For instance, traveling across the country for a meeting that could happen over Zoom? Why would I do that, given the carbon emissions associated with long-distance travel, not to mention the wear and tear on my body? This season of pandemic includes both interruption to that which we might consider normal, and the introduction of a new normal, some of which might actually stick, if and when the old normal returns. The season is changing, and it is also changing us.

Traditional leadership practices include certain responsibilities, no matter the field: working with a community of stakeholders to cast a vision; planning, implementing, managing, evaluating, and improving the community's work; and then revisiting the vision to assess progress. Visioning, according to this typical modern and postmodern set of leadership practices, serves to bookend a set of conventional practices: we envision before we carry out our work, and we return to the vision to assess our effectiveness.

What happens when we take the bookends away? When we are in an in-between time, visioning can still take place, but it is dramatically less useful. It can even be a source of frustration and discouragement. Our imaginations sputter and moan at the strain of coming up with a mental picture with too many variables to take into consideration. What is a leader to do?

Beaumont commends to readers a leadership strategy for a liminal season that borrows from Ronald Heifetz's metaphor of turning up and turning down the heat on a stove. Heifetz writes, in *Leadership Without Easy Answers*[25] and elsewhere, that leaders must present change to constituents at a rate—a temperature—they can tolerate, neither undercooking nor getting burned. In a liminal season, Beaumont writes that leaders turn up the heat by provoking constituents to recognize that times have changed and that the old ways do not work anymore. They draw attention to unresolved issues, delegate responsibility in ways that push constituents beyond their comfort zones, bring conflict to the surface, and treat every obstacle like an opportunity to gather strength for the journey. Leaders then provide respite from the anxiety they provoke by framing issues, using time limits, reclaiming some of the hardest work for the leaders themselves to handle, and building up early successes as well as communal confidence.

The following is an example of a change on which I am working now, where Beaumont's metaphor of turning the heat up and down can come to life. The seminary I serve has a long tradition of teaching students about social justice through cross-cultural immersion. In recent years, however, the educational model has begun to show its limitations. When a group of students goes from one global setting to another, they shift into guest mode, but their movements mirror those of conquerors of past days. Some students spoke of feeling like voyeurs when visiting parts of the world struck by extreme poverty; more recently, the term "poverty porn" entered students' vocabulary. When "we" go visit "them," questions come up about what makes us "we," and what makes others "other." What vision for social justice were we presenting students by sending them on trips? It became clear in 2019 that it had been too long since we had asked that question.

Why 2019? Because two trips in a row included tension and conflict within groups, and the pattern became impossible to ignore. The conflicts were not straightforward and did not center around some of the difficult ethical issues I name above. Students complained, for example, that the schedule on the trips was too grueling, the days too long. These are not lazy students by any stretch of the imagination, so I wondered, "Where is that complaint coming from?" Students had conflicts with one another, group leaders had conflicts with one another, and group leaders had conflicts with students. Participants suggested that not enough work had been done in advance of the trips to ensure group cohesion, which might have been one of the problems, but I began to see signs that individuals were becoming symptom-bearers of a broken educational model.

The last trip before we put the program on hold brought together every difficult dynamic one could imagine. The trip was to Kenya, and more than half the students were African-American, while the two faculty leaders were white men and the chaplain to the trip a white woman. Although I had extensive conversations with the group leaders about how to mitigate the power dynamic likely to ensue, it pulled at the group's cohesion from the very first pre-travel meeting. I attempted every intervention within my power before and during the trip, but tensions in the group led to damaged relationships. Something new needed to happen. The steps that ensued blended those that turned up and turned down the heat, sometimes with one step doing a little bit of both.

1. I both fielded concerns from those upset by the whole ordeal (tended to the heat), and I also checked in with those who had been on the trip but had not been as upset, whose judgment I trusted (cooled off).

2. I learned that a respected student leader, who had not been on the trip but had been on the previous trip, had suggested to other students that our school was ignoring problems, which was not true, but an understandable impression given our attempts at mitigation were not happening on a public stage. I sought out the student leader and set the record straight. (Heating up through confrontation and cooling off through getting to a new shared understanding of what actually happened.)

3. I consulted with my board and trusted administrative colleagues. (Cooling off.)

4. I terminated our school's partnership with the travel seminar organization that had not sufficiently adjusted in light of our feedback (heating up) and put the whole travel seminar program on hiatus (cooling off).

5. I convened a task force made up of representatives of different stakeholders to map out a future for social justice and immersion-style education. (Moderating the temperature for the longer-term.)

Each of these steps took what felt initially like a blast of heat, moved us into a pattern of heating and cooling, and landed us at a lower temperature we could sustain through a longer-term discernment process. By balancing heating and cooling, we are on a path toward a new, better form of social justice education program that disrupts the *status quo* but will result eventually in a life-giving new way.

Later in this book, I will recommend a different kind of force to hold traditional leadership practices—planning, implementation, and management—together: tension resulting from intentionality. For now, however, I propose that, in a liminal time, discernment is a more useful leadership practice than visioning. Visioning is of course possible, and it bears similarities to discernment, but given the indefinite nature of our culture's sojourn in liminality, we must not focus solely on what we will do on the other side of it. This liminality has substance—its own nature—and we need to learn to live in it.

Visioning is about looking to the future, and discernment relates to understanding the nature of the present moment. Here is a visioning exercise I have occasionally used with groups of stakeholders: the Polaroid picture exercise. I ask participants to close their eyes and imagine a future where their community is fully alive. I invite them to take time to notice details and specifics about their imagined future, and then snap an imaginary Polaroid. After they open their eyes, I either encourage them to draw their picture, or describe it to the person next to them.

Another visioning exercise I have found effective when working with groups involves a process of focusing a community on the impact members want to have on the world. I ask the question, "If this community could only accomplish five things, what would they be?" Each participant in the visioning exercise then creates five cards. After doing so, I ask them to pick a partner and pose the question again: "If we could only accomplish five things..."

and the pair must choose five from their ten. Then the pairs become groups of four ("Still, only five priorities!" I say, and groans erupt), and so-on, until the whole gathered community has had to select five hoped-for areas of focus, all together. Laughter and playful arm-wrestling help the group to loosen the bonds of the high expectations they carry. They work together, and boiling ideas down to five is always easier than they thought it would be. Here is what is great about these exercises: they promote conversation, ownership, and positivity. The shortcomings surely leap to the eye: everyone's imagination is different, and although this knowledge itself is helpful for the group to see and understand, it is difficult to bridge different visions. More troublesome in a liminal time is the fact that the imagined future might be very, very far away. What are we to do *now*? How can we find energy to motivate us toward the future when the future is increasingly nebulous, more likely to provoke anxiety than excitement?

In making a distinction between visioning and discernment, a person could easily jump to the conclusion that the difference is God. Visioning might be an activity we associate with secular, even for-profit, organizations, and discernment with Christian life and leadership. In fact, both can be God-centered or human-centered, depending on the exercise's orientation. A faith community's visioning can and should center on the community discerning God's will for it and God's call to it. A corporation's visioning relates to secular forms of success, such as profitability and financial sustainability. Corporations' visions could be wise or unwise, worthy or unworthy, ethical or unethical, but ultimately the source of the vision is the leaders themselves, not the leaders' interpretation of God's will.

The true distinction between visioning and discernment, therefore, relates to imagination and time. Visioning requires picturing something new that has never been before (imagination) in the future (time). Discernment attends to what is happening here and now. Visioning can motivate creativity, but it is risky, in that building something never-before-seen might not work. Discernment is risky too, in that attending to what is happening in the here-and-now might show us that which is painful for us to see. In Christian visioning, we pray, "God, show us what you imagine for us, your creation." In Christian discernment, we ask, "God, help me to see the truth the way you see it: the truth in and around your creation." Discernment requires less interpretation of God's imagination and more honesty about who we really are, and what our world is and is becoming.

The leaders' role in casting a vision includes not just the leader listening for God's voice, asking God to reveal God's imagination for creation, but it requires bringing people together for communal imagining. The Polaroid picture exercise described above marks just one of hundreds of possible ways to bring to the surface the community's innate knowledge of God's hopes for us. I come from a branch of the Christian tree that values the insights of all in the faith community, giving due respect but little privilege to clergy and much credence to voices at the margins that might be excluded from other communal conversations. Therefore, having a good process for visioning, one that does not allow any single perspective to take over, is important and often the responsibility of the leader.

NOTES

22. Putnam and Campbell, *American Grace.*
23. Beaumont, *How to Lead When You Don't Know Where You're Going.*
24. Ibid., 2.
25. Heifetz, *Leadership without Easy Answers.*

▪ 6 ▪

DISCERNMENT FROM MULTIPLE PERSPECTIVES

We live in a noisy and distracting world. Leaders must find ways to garner the levels of attention needed to discern what is happening in the individual human heart, in the community, and in the world. To design approaches to communal discernment, leaders need theoretical frameworks to guide them, yet while theories about leading toward a vision are abundant, theories for helping a community discern are less so. Perhaps leadership literature has worked under the assumption that leaders cast visions, and discernment is for individuals and their spiritual directors. With a broader understanding of the nature of discernment, leaders can craft interventions that help the community see their setting and themselves differently.

Let us return to Susan Beaumont's description of the nature of a liminal time. Amidst seasons of complexity and change, where different people have widely varied interpretations of reality and at the same time face overwhelming challenges, capacity for discernment is the new leadership superpower. Beaumont writes that the markers of liminality for which we must watch as leaders include disengagement and disorientation.[26] The "dis-" prefix suggests that the leader must watch for something not-there, an absence of behavior rather than its identifiable presence. Clearly, it is easier to see upset than disengagement. Another set of signs Beaumont names relates to leadership burnout. "Normal" starts to feel irrelevant and unattainable, and keeping up the old practices that ensured the past status quo become unbearably draining. Like disengagement and disorientation, burnout is subtle and slow, and only discernment will help us know its cause.

I have long heard the expression, whose original origins are unknown at least to me, "You have to read it to lead it." In other words, a leader must have a clear-eyed view of the reality of their settings to make good choices. At the seminary I serve, one of our six core competencies for ministry is "perspicacity," or the capacity to both interpret a situation in a context and forge a strategy for functioning well within that situation and context. Our program's educational leaders and students alike tried mightily to find a less intimidating word than "perspicacity," which is hard to say and borderline-pretentious, but ultimately, the word captured the blend of seeing what is needed and considering right actions. Through discernment practices, leaders can become more perspicacious, even aspiring to excellence in it.

I first took an interest in the spiritual practice of discernment because of my fascination with *vocational* discernment. Vocation, with the Latin root *"vocare,"* or "to call," is the theological concept that God has an intention for that which God creates. To uncover it, we must listen for God's voice, and sometimes listening requires quieting that which is not of God so we can hear. Vocational discernment for an individual might relate to career, family choices, and creative enterprises. For an organization, vocation relates to mission.

As a student, and then as a campus minister and administrator in higher education, witnessing and being a part of the process through which students discovered a major, curated their courses and experiences, and eventually found their calling was a source of amazement for me. I decided to explore the process by minoring in career psychology in my doctoral program and writing my dissertation on vocational discernment programs supported by grants from the Lilly Endowment, Inc. Over the years, I have gathered a number of theoretical frameworks for discernment, and here I will share my top three.

TRAIT-FACTOR CONGRUENCE

The field of career psychology, whose language pervades ordinary conversation about discernment, relies on the concept of finding a match. We are born a particular "shape" as relates to our personalities, talents, and interests. We can modify that shape through education and life experience. We then look for life partners, companions, and careers that fit our shape. The concept of trait-factor congruence captures what is usually simply assumed: we are at our happiest when we find in our outer lives a match with our inner lives. "Trait" describes an attribute of a particular human being, like an interest in animals, or a knack for numbers. "Factor" describes a similar attribute in a professional field. The person whose trait is a love for animals might find the factors they seek in veterinary medicine, for instance, or farming. "Congruence," a term we might remember from middle school geometry, signifies a mirroring shape. The human being has a shape, as does the career field, and through trial and error, we discover which of our traits match up with which of a field's factors until we find our congruent counterpart.

Trial and error as a style of discernment can assist not just individual decision-making but institutional leadership. Leaders help communities and institutions to define their missions and refine their identities. Then, leaders guide them as they choose where to place their energies. Innovation requires trying new activities, but leaders do a disservice to institutions when they make efforts akin to throwing spaghetti against a wall to see if it sticks. Trying everything drains institutions and confuses them in their quest for a clear identity. One communal approach to trial and error is the implementation of pilot initiatives: the organization defines its identity and then attempts programmatic expressions of that identity at a small scale, minimizing risk and cost. Pilot initiatives should include evaluative practices that determine whether a continuation or expansion of the program makes sense. The good news: even communities most resistant to change and risk are likely to be more open to pilot initiatives than new programs, and they are in turn more open to new directions following successful pilot experiments.

FORGETTING OURSELVES ON PURPOSE

Seeking a career or partner who is a match for us requires great intentionality and hard work. First, we need to get to know ourselves. Then, we have to discover what the world has to offer. Both processes take years, even decades. Brian Mahan, in his book *Forgetting Ourselves on Purpose: Vocation and the Ethics of Ambition*,[27] offers a different and less effortful method for discernment.

Mahan argues that we learn best who we are by considering where our mind goes when it wanders, and the activities in which we engage where we lose track of time. Mahan writes that we experience a series of "epiphanies of recruitment" in our lives, where we make dramatic and rapid progress toward knowing where our hearts are. We must attend to the difference between yearning for lauds and accolades versus yearning to feel authentically whole. Once we do that, however, our work is to discern that which feels so natural to us by way of occupation that doing it feels like self-actualization rather than striving.

At this point in my life, I see the deep wisdom of Mahan's theory, but when I first read it, I found it counterintuitive to what I had been told my whole life: striving is everything. My first date with the person who became my spouse spanned sixteen hours and felt like a minute. I lose myself in program development for students and do not wish a second away. But I was taught for so long that discernment involved *work* that the value of self-forgetting took me some convincing. Because it defies the assumption that the best way to discern is to work to find a match, Mahan offers exercises to help a person discover their vocation—or calling—through forgetting themselves. He commends keeping a "distraction diary," for example, where we jot down where our mind has gone when it wanders, rather than when our minds are exerting themselves in the efforts of navigation.

An institutional expression of Mahan's style of discernment looks something like a return to basics. As organizations evolve over time, adjusting to circumstances and changing contexts, it is easy for them to adopt a stance of striving. Doing what feels natural and easy might run counter to the organization's very mission if the institution originated out of resistance to the status quo and desire for cultural change. Forgetting ourselves on purpose might involve deciding to consciously stop doing that which feels hard, and then see what happens. Finding it impossible to fill a position? Cancel the search. Unable to find volunteers to staff a certain committee? Disband it. No one showing up to midweek services? Do away with them. Of course, these acts of abandonment must be quickly followed with reflective practice. What does it mean about our future that, when left to its own physics, the organization wants to go this way, not that way? God's will is in the letting go as much as in the striving.

THREE KEYS[28]

Father Michael Himes of Boston College created a video for students as part of that school's Program for the Theological Exploration of Vocation, funded by the Lilly Endowment, in the early 2000s. Himes presents three key questions for discerning what God intends for us to do with our lives: does this activity bring me joy? Am I good at it? And does someone need me to do it?

Himes is careful to define joy as a deep sense of satisfaction, beyond happiness. Joy inspires us and enables us to sustain the ups and downs that come with any endeavor worthy of our commitment. He defines that at which we are good as something we cannot know alone, but where we rely on feedback from others. Finally, he is pragmatic in asking the question of whether what we are doing meets a genuine need in the world. Himes's three questions blend the individual and communal dimensions of vocation in a way that connects callings with service without losing the desires of the called person.

Organizations engage in asking these three questions every time they work together on a mission statement or strategic plan. Mission statements sometimes lack specificity and focus, which is understandable when one considers the changing times and their related uncertainties. Strategic plans rarely provide actual guidance for where to say no and yes as opportunities emerge, and they can be full of statements that mean nothing in the absence of reference to the past. To say we will do everything we used to do, "more" and "better," ties missions to the past.

Institutions do well to consider Himes's three questions when framing their purposes. Institutional "joy" might mean different things to different people, but what causes institutional leaders to sense deep satisfaction is a more helpful guide than "more and better." Whether a particular institution is the best one to carry out particular work, or good at that work, is an excellent question rarely asked. What the world needs from organizations changes with the generations, and again, whether the world needs what the institution provides is perhaps the most relevant question to consider when engaged in planning.

My own institution went through a major change in 2016. The change had been brewing for a long time, as had the problems that necessitated change. Andover Newton was a free-standing seminary with a beautiful, massive campus in a high-priced suburb of Boston. The campus suffered from deferred maintenance that caused occasional scares, including steam pipe leaks and brownouts due to the aging electric grid. Enrollment was declining in logical sync with membership in the churches with which we were most closely aligned. Students were taking on too much debt. Donors were nervous about the school's future to the point where they were holding back on their giving. The school suffered crisis after crisis on top of these chronic conditions, and each one consumed more energy than we had to spare. It was as though we were in a small boat on the ocean: every wave tossed us about.

For my first ten years at Andover Newton, the approach leaders took was to try everything: unlikely mergers with strange bedfellows, new programmatic directions, renters on the campus, and new partners buying up our campus from the edges inward. All these efforts felt like throwing the kitchen sink at the problem of unsustainability. In retrospect, I realize we had to do that: throw everything, including the kitchen sink, at our untenable situation; had we not, perhaps we would not have believed later, when times got toughest, that we had no other choice than the one we pursued.

During a strategic planning process that felt very much like a last-ditch effort, even though none of us were willing to name that reality given our anxieties, the "more" and "better" approach gave way to clarity that our school's founding mission, to educate leaders for faith communities, was the plumb line through all we had ever been and done. We were better at it than our peers, and students came to us knowing that. When presented with options for the future, we chose the one where we could focus in on what it takes to educate leaders for locally governed congregations, and that renewal of purpose gave us focus and energy.

The reasons for which we had broadened our scope over time, adding programs that departed from our core mission to educate pastors, had less to do with the changing context of ministry, even though that context was indeed changing. How do I know? Because if we had really been paying attention to the context, we would have radically decreased the size of our enrollment of degree-earners and provided nondegree education to church leaders not preparing for full-time service. Why had we not taken that direction? Tuition dependency. We had contorted ourselves and needed to un-contort ourselves. What gave us joy, where our gifts lay, and what the world needed from us more than anyone else resulted in our becoming a smaller, embedded school that works with a subset of theological students oriented to faith community leadership.

There was no moment I remember in our institution's discernment where we used the language of joy, but we did honor our gifts and heritage in making our move. Joy had gotten lost over years of anxiety and is only just beginning to reemerge. Fear of letting down our constituents and ancestors created a cacophony not easily overcome. Anyone who has been in leadership in an existentially threatened organization knows that simply tuning out the noise is not an option except for the most compartmentalized among us. Practices of discernment can help filter out some of the noise by providing a discipline and routine. Even more importantly, leaders must rely on God and remember that God was the only One in control all along.

NOTES

26. Beaumont, *How to Lead When You Don't Know Where You're Going*, 2.

27. Brian Mahan, *Forgetting Ourselves on Purpose: Vocation and the Ethics of Ambition* (San Francisco: Jossey-Bass, 2002).

28. Rev. Michael Himes, "Three Key Questions," posted April 20, 2016, YouTube video, https://www.youtube.com/watch?v=P-4lKCENdnw.

∎ 7 ∎

DYNAMIC DISCERNMENT REVISITED

L eadership in the twenty-first century requires all the old management ways—planning, managing, evaluating, improving—*plus* a capacity for discernment unlike anything we have needed before. Those who write about leadership have long insisted that the capacity to read a context and diagnose a situation is a crucial step, more art than science. Increasingly diverse communities challenge our capacity to read and diagnose, however, as all of us are limited by our own perspectives and experiences. As Michael Himes says in his "Three Keys" video,[29] we cannot read people like books, because they are people, not books. Add to that natural human complexity the fact that we come from different backgrounds and cultures, and the assumptions we are likely to make when trying to read others can be downright damaging.

The three discernment practices named here—trait-factor congruence, forgetting ourselves on purpose, and "three keys"—

demonstrate that we and our contexts are complex. In my book *Dynamic Discernment: Reason, Emotion, and Power in Change Leadership*,[30] I provide some guidance for choosing a leadership style based on a community's presenting dynamic. I define "reason" as the sense-making work of leadership, which should enable communities to understand the problem the leader is seeing and trying to solve, see the connections between the leadership strategy and the leaders' actions, and buy into the new direction.

If reason is what is missing and needed, the community might present itself as confused, with all the anxiety confusion brings. When the leader hears complaints about poor communication or gets the sense that the community does not understand the rationale behind a change underway, they can engage in the leadership practices of planning and teaching, and the community may relax and get onboard. The good news is that most of us already know how to make plans and explain our choices, so reason is a dynamic that can improve quickly. The other two dynamics I describe in the book are less easily grasped.

If the presenting dynamic is emotional in nature, the signs might be less easy to see and read. The leader gets the impression that tensions are running high, but direct questions about body language or clipped responses get the leader nowhere. Upset crops up in one part of the organization, even though the dysfunction that seems to require attention is taking place in an entirely different part of the institution. A person who is normally calm and easygoing has a full-on temper tantrum in a meeting for no apparent reason. Emotional systems theory tells us that emotion does not belong to individuals. Communities create shared pools of emotion whose levels rise and fall. That which contributes to an emotional dynamic, and where that dynamic finds expression, are often seemingly unrelated to one another. The work of untangling an unhealthy emotional system makes for a longer haul.

Two examples of the methodical, long-term work necessary for building a healthy emotional system include, first, the leadership task of aligning responsibility with power to *carry out* responsibility. Such alignment reduces the stress that comes with operating outside our mandate and overfunctioning. Restructuring an organization's staff so that everyone on the team has a portfolio of responsibilities of their own, and appropriate authority to carry out those responsibilities under scrutiny, but without micromanagement, is one example of locating power and responsibility in close proximity to each other. For example, the seminary administrator at my school assists me with administrative duties as part of her responsibilities, but I do not refer to her as my assistant.

Second, amidst unhealthy emotional systems, the leader must attend to their self-differentiation. The leader must exhibit a clear sense of where they end and others begin, thus modeling that our emotions are our own responsibilities. Self-differentiation is not selfishness; it is the honest exhibiting that we are all separate beings who must take care of ourselves and take responsibility for our own actions and feelings. When leaders model healthy detachment and self-containment, others follow suit, embodying the notion that we have emotions, but emotions do not have us. The Covid-19 pandemic has brought every conceivable form of anxiety to our emotional lives, from fear of death (from Covid) to fear of disappointing others (like children who cannot freely play). Leaders must name those anxieties without succumbing to them, acknowledging human experience while demonstrating resilience. To model thoughtfulness but not give oneself over to emotions can be tiring, and the pandemic has endured for a long time. Yet communal anxieties can become even more overpowering when leaders stoke the fire rather than turning down the heat.

Most elusive of all is the dynamic that results from imbalances of power. I write in *Dynamic Discernment* that power creates the most challenging of the three dynamics explored because power, by nature, knows how to hide. It preserves itself by pretending it does not exist. Whereas confusion tells us that reason is the dynamic that requires a leader's attention, and unexplained upset tells us something is off in the emotional system, problems in the power dynamic can be downright imperceptible. Perhaps the leader will preside over a community decision that seems to be final, only to find it overturned through a parking lot conversation with a small cabal of influential stakeholders. Maybe a search process for a new executive will lean in the direction of the will of a constituent with control over resources, without anyone in the group saying aloud that they are bending to that person's will and perhaps even without their awareness that they are bending at all.

In *Dynamic Discernment*, I propose long- and short-term approaches to working through unhealthy power dynamics. Power inequality is natural, and consciousness is possible. The long haul is the journey toward liberation. Liberation Theology, a way of thinking about God and faith with origins in the agrarian communities of Central and South America, has at its core a desire to break free of the shackles of oppression, not just for the oppressed but for the oppressor. A typical human response to having been oppressed is that people wish to overthrow those who force them to work, suffer, and conform. The likely result of overthrowing an overlord is that the oppressed would simply become the new overlord, however, without liberation for all. The alternative is a process of what liberation-centered educator Paulo Freire called "conscientization," where all become conscious of how power is infecting their relationships and hindering freedom. Neither oppressed nor oppressor can break the cycle keeping all in bondage without awareness of the invisible forces shaping and distorting their lives. Yet conscientization takes years or generations, and leadership decisions about how to work within a complex and dysfunctional power dynamic must take place in real time. Therefore, I borrow concepts from the fields of engineering and community organizing (talk about strange bedfellows!) in describing an approach that calls upon those with grassroots power and those with top-down, authorized power to find common areas of interest and work on them. Working together fosters relationships, and relationships foster consciousness. Rather than attacking power head on, only to have it run for the shadows, I propose focusing on a common problem and allowing awareness of each other's humanity to emerge along with ideas, solutions, and a sense of shared purpose.

The Greater Boston Interfaith Organization, a community organizing collective in Massachusetts, brings religious communities together to consider actions on common problems. Examples of GBIO initiatives include health care, support for the elderly, and curbing gun violence. Their work on gun violence, in particular, has embodied what seems to the naked eye to be acceptance of gun culture. They do not talk about making guns illegal; rather, they pressure gunmakers to incorporate safety features. To watch my clergy colleague demonstrate firearm technologies ("See! Only the person wearing the encoded bracelet can cock the gun!") was jarring, but it also exemplified working within the framework of power dynamics. Gun companies and clergy activists share a goal: reduce murders. Many of GBIO's leaders have joined the National Rifle Association in order to know what they were facing and engage in conversation with those who have the power to reduce gun violence more quickly than activists could when disengaged. In my own work in theological education, power is more subtle than that held by the NRA. Liberal Christians do not like to acknowledge that they even have power, let alone power they might abuse. I have participated in a number of negotiations related to institutional partnerships and mergers. Most of them have failed, so I have learned a great deal about how not acknowledging power dynamics can scuttle good ideas. To anyone who asks, I am happy to share what has killed mergers that would have been good for both institutions if mission were all that mattered: legal issues and money issues. Both bring out a competitive dynamic in mergers, where neither institution wants to lose independence (legally) or give up access to resources (money). The institutional partnership in which I now participate was rendered simpler and easier by virtue of the fact that one institution was extremely strong, the other fragile, so there was no ambiguity about who had the upper hand. The stronger institution has never behaved as an aggressor, but knowing that it could do so at any moment made for fewer surprises when power reared its head.

I worried when I wrote about power in *Dynamic Discernment* that I would get serious pushback from my liberal colleagues. What I propose by way of a strategy—cooperation around shared interests without meaningfully disrupting oppressive structures— is tantamount to accepting that oppressors will oppress, after all. Instead, I received appreciation for acknowledging that power is elusive and, when uncovered, not always worth fighting. What engineers call "critical path" management is a form of cooperation between form and function, where the purpose is to engineer solutions around what people are likely to do anyway. For instance, a person designing a new hiking trail through the woods might look first for where the ground is worn down by the footfalls of animals. A critical-path approach to liberation calls on the oppressed and the oppressors to collaborate where they can, preserving energy for transformation and liberation that will come in due time, as they come to trust one another.

In her work on leadership amidst liminality, Susan Beaumont suggests three concepts that I believe can be fruitfully coupled with the three dynamics I describe in *Dynamic Discernment*. First, she employs the Latin term, *communitas*. The communitas of an institution is its transcendent nature and essence, not to be confused with the community as it stands in a specific moment in time. One illustration I have used for describing a communitas is that shared among the alumni and alumnae of a school. They are not part of the school of the moment, but are rather part of its communitas and can at times have passionate feelings about the school due to a deep sense of belonging. Alums can sometimes annoy educational leaders, in that they do not realize how much the institution has changed since they were in the student body and decry change that the leader believes good and necessary. Yet the leader is wise to draw attention to communitas and promote its celebration. Leaders, constituents, and programs come and go, but a strong sense of communitas knits organizations together at a deeper level that can be retrieved in in-between times as a source of direction and motivation.

A second concept Beaumont describes and explores is what she calls "the trickster." Many who write about emotional systems explore the behavior of saboteurs who come out of the woodwork to resist even wise and life-giving institutional change. Beaumont offers a slightly different perspective from systems theorists, describing tricksters as ones who seek to throw wrenches into the gears of change not out of fear and protectiveness of the status quo, but out of hunger for the drama that accompanies liminality. Tricksters do not resist change; rather, they stir the proverbial pot in order to make liminality last longer. Tricksters thus confuse communities. Wise leaders encourage their constituents to inhabit liminality in a posture of discernment, watching and waiting for creativity to blossom and bear fruit. Tricksters postpone needed emergence that would threaten the liminality that is feeding an unhealthy need within them. Tricksters delay progress; discerners who allow something new to be born are entirely different. Leaders must identify which one is happening—delay or discernment— and move tricksters away from the controls guiding the ship.

For many years, I kept a bumper sticker over my desk that said, "Jesus is coming; look busy." The third concept from Beaumont's work on leadership amidst liminality is one we could call the "'look busy' principle." Beaumont writes that we fear liminal seasons, as they always begin with grief. Whenever we have something and lose it, we grieve, even if we did not want that which we lost anymore, and even if what we had was actively doing us harm. Therefore, out of natural human fear of pain, we resist entering liminality, the in-between time after what was and before what will become. We also wish to rush out of liminality as soon as possible so that we can replace what we had and stanch the bleeding of grief's accompanying sadness.

The problem with rushing out of liminality, and into that which is new, is that the new must emerge; it cannot be forced or rushed. The leader can guide the work of discernment to ensure that, when emergence happens, they recognize it. The great challenge is helping the community stay with the questions, rather than forcing answers. Leaders must help the community linger amidst uncertainty and feel safe there. This leadership task—creating an environment in which lingering is bearable—runs counter to what most leaders' communities expect of them, which is to take action and make feelings of uncertainty go away. In order for communities to do the creative work of imagining a new future, they must trust their leaders. In the absence of such trust, they will not be able to let go of the old, or they will rush to the new as if it were a lifeboat.

Therefore, leaders must look busy. They must attend to the conventional practices of planning, implementation, and management in visible ways. By looking busy—and with no shortage of tasks, we actually are busy—the community remains confident that the leader is engaged and paying attention. The leader might have been selected to drive the institution into the future, but the leader will only succeed if the community together discerns its new direction, which requires stillness. We manage the community's disappointment that we cannot put a simple and immediate end to liminality by showing up, by showing the community the tasks we *can* and *have* managed. Then, the leader works to cultivate a sense of realness—authenticity amidst uncertainty—that causes others to feel they can be real as well. The community then can face the challenge of uncertainty amidst liminality while simultaneously wholly human and wholly open to the voice of the divine.

NOTES

29. Himes, "Three Key Questions."
30. Drummond, *Dynamic Discernment.*

8

IRONIES OVER LINEARITY

In the life of faith and the life of leadership, juxtapositions abound. As described above, Beaumont writes about the importance of leaders balancing authenticity with action, presence, and busyness. Elsewhere in her writing on liminality, she contrasts advocacy versus attending, striving versus surrender. Ron Heifetz writes how leaders must move fluidly from the dance floor to the balcony: from the midst of the fray to a posture of observation. Christian spiritual teachers from across the centuries write about detecting the difference between the performative and approval-craving false self, and the self we know as Christ-in-us. An easy but mistaken approach to these dualisms would be to say that one is good, and the other is bad. We must befriend both, in order that we might know ourselves and lead with the knowledge that is available to us.

So far, this book has provided readers with a backdrop to a new leadership theory for a liminal time. The next chapter will introduce the theory itself, but before then, the background needs one more dimension: the role of irony in leadership.

▪ 8 ▪

IRONIES OVER LINEARITY

In the life of faith and the life of leadership, juxtapositions abound. As described above, Beaumont writes about the importance of leaders balancing authenticity with action, presence, and busyness. Elsewhere in her writing on liminality, she contrasts advocacy versus attending, striving versus surrender. Ron Heifetz writes how leaders must move fluidly from the dance floor to the balcony: from the midst of the fray to a posture of observation. Christian spiritual teachers from across the centuries write about detecting the difference between the performative and approval-craving false self, and the self we know as Christ-in-us. An easy but mistaken approach to these dualisms would be to say that one is good, and the other is bad. We must befriend both, in order that we might know ourselves and lead with the knowledge that is available to us.

So far, this book has provided readers with a backdrop to a new leadership theory for a liminal time. The next chapter will introduce the theory itself, but before then, the background needs one more dimension: the role of irony in leadership.

person designing a new hiking trail through the woods might look first for where the ground is worn down by the footfalls of animals. A critical-path approach to liberation calls on the oppressed and the oppressors to collaborate where they can, preserving energy for transformation and liberation that will come in due time, as they come to trust one another.

In her work on leadership amidst liminality, Susan Beaumont suggests three concepts that I believe can be fruitfully coupled with the three dynamics I describe in *Dynamic Discernment*. First, she employs the Latin term, *communitas*. The communitas of an institution is its transcendent nature and essence, not to be confused with the community as it stands in a specific moment in time. One illustration I have used for describing a communitas is that shared among the alumni and alumnae of a school. They are not part of the school of the moment, but are rather part of its communitas and can at times have passionate feelings about the school due to a deep sense of belonging. Alums can sometimes annoy educational leaders, in that they do not realize how much the institution has changed since they were in the student body and decry change that the leader believes good and necessary. Yet the leader is wise to draw attention to communitas and promote its celebration. Leaders, constituents, and programs come and go, but a strong sense of communitas knits organizations together at a deeper level that can be retrieved in in-between times as a source of direction and motivation.

A second concept Beaumont describes and explores is what she calls "the trickster." Many who write about emotional systems explore the behavior of saboteurs who come out of the woodwork to resist even wise and life-giving institutional change. Beaumont offers a slightly different perspective from systems theorists, describing tricksters as ones who seek to throw wrenches into the gears of change not out of fear and protectiveness of the status quo, but out of hunger for the drama that accompanies liminality. Tricksters do not resist change; rather, they stir the proverbial pot in order to make liminality last longer. Tricksters thus confuse communities. Wise leaders encourage their constituents to inhabit liminality in a posture of discernment, watching and waiting for creativity to blossom and bear fruit. Tricksters postpone needed emergence that would threaten the liminality that is feeding an unhealthy need within them. Tricksters delay progress; discerners who allow something new to be born are entirely different. Leaders must identify which one is happening—delay or discernment— and move tricksters away from the controls guiding the ship.

For many years, I kept a bumper sticker over my desk that said, "Jesus is coming; look busy." The third concept from Beaumont's work on leadership amidst liminality is one we could call the "'look busy' principle." Beaumont writes that we fear liminal seasons, as they always begin with grief. Whenever we have something and lose it, we grieve, even if we did not want that which we lost anymore, and even if what we had was actively doing us harm. Therefore, out of natural human fear of pain, we resist entering liminality, the in-between time after what was and before what will become. We also wish to rush out of liminality as soon as possible so that we can replace what we had and stanch the bleeding of grief's accompanying sadness.

The problem with rushing out of liminality, and into that which is new, is that the new must emerge; it cannot be forced or rushed. The leader can guide the work of discernment to ensure that, when emergence happens, they recognize it. The great challenge is helping the community stay with the questions, rather than forcing

answers. Leaders must help the community linger amidst uncertainty and feel safe there. This leadership task—creating an environment in which lingering is bearable—runs counter to what most leaders' communities expect of them, which is to take action and make feelings of uncertainty go away. In order for communities to do the creative work of imagining a new future, they must trust their leaders. In the absence of such trust, they will not be able to let go of the old, or they will rush to the new as if it were a lifeboat.

Therefore, leaders must look busy. They must attend to the conventional practices of planning, implementation, and management in visible ways. By looking busy—and with no shortage of tasks, we actually are busy—the community remains confident that the leader is engaged and paying attention. The leader might have been selected to drive the institution into the future, but the leader will only succeed if the community together discerns its new direction, which requires stillness. We manage the community's disappointment that we cannot put a simple and immediate end to liminality by showing up, by showing the community the tasks w *can* and *have* managed. Then, the leader works to cultivate a ser of realness—authenticity amidst uncertainty—that causes oth to feel they can be real as well. The community then can face challenge of uncertainty amidst liminality while simultane wholly human and wholly open to the voice of the divine.

NOTES

29. Himes, "Three Key Questions."
30. Drummond, *Dynamic Discernment*.

At the end of the previous section, I describe some dualisms that characterize liminality. Leaders receive a message from the wider culture that people of integrity are entirely consistent, all the time. By that definition, however, no one who is engaged in their community, and who takes their responsibilities seriously, has integrity. Leaders, just like all human beings, must come to terms with the fact that they cannot be consistent in settings as complex as twenty-first century communities. Leaders can be fair, and they can have an inner compass, but living out their values by necessity looks different in different situations.

Consider, for example, the leadership skills needed to bring about innovation in a religious setting. In *Amazing Grace*,[31] the authors describe four forms such innovation might take:

- A *new medium*, such as online worship during a pandemic.

- A *new form*, such as a Sunday-morning-worshipping congregation going on a weekend-long retreat.

- New *practices*, such as a time for personal sharing during a sermon in the pews.

- *Tradition reintroduction*, such as labyrinth walking or contemplative prayer.

All such innovations require leadership that pushes past discomfort, and pushing past discomfort requires no small amount of playacting. The leader who seems uncomfortable and hesitant having their feet washed in a foot-washing ceremony, reintroduced into Maundy Thursday services, will do little to help the congregation embrace something new to them. Is the leader who pretends for the sake of normalization a fake and fraud? No; that leader is doing the job that needs to be done.

Perhaps it is part of the human condition that we create dualisms where we do not need them and fail to allow for irony. Among dualisms we do not need, for instance, is a false dichotomy between spiritual leadership and political or business leadership. Though their respective bottom lines are different, leadership in different settings is far more similar than different. The real contrasts lie within the leaders themselves and their comfort level with the irony required by strategic pivoting. This irony is anything but two-faced. While two-faced leaders and leaders comfortable with irony are sometimes hard to distinguish from one another, the latter are more likely to get a community through a liminal time. On the outside, the choices of a person who—out of insecure self-absorption—changes positions constantly to curry favor and the person who adjusts based on the needs of the context look an awful lot alike. The difference between them? Maturity.

Consider the diagram on page 81:

In the year we were engaged to be married, my spouse and I took a course together at the Harvard Graduate School of Education. The course was called Adult Development, and the instructor was Robert Kegan. The diagram below is my interpretation, many years later, of the guiding theoretical framework for the course.

At the bottom of the diagram, we see the beginning of the life cycle: our birth. Even our birth results from development. We begin in our mothers' wombs, and when we are too big for the space, we become uncomfortable to the point where hormonal messages tell our mother's bodies that it is time for us to be born. That pattern—getting uncomfortable and having to make a change because we have grown—drives our development throughout our lives.

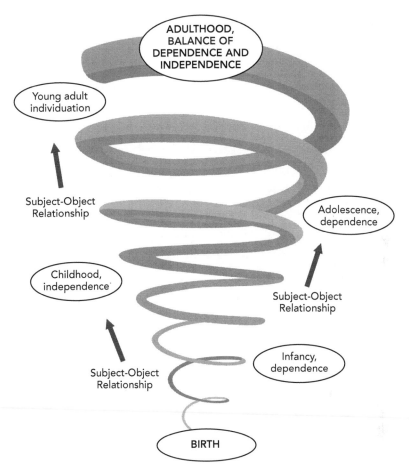

The five stages of development Kegan describes are ones that many other scholars of developmental theory have adopted and expanded upon: childhood, adolescence, young adulthood, middle adulthood, and a generative or stagnant period in older age. Other developmental theorists, such as Erik Erikson and James Fowler, focused on different dimensions of a stage theory of development: Erikson on education, Fowler on spirituality. Kegan was, when I took his course, focused on the adult years. Since that time, he has taken a strong interest in leadership. Still, the lesson from Kegan I find most useful was the one I encountered first: the development spiral. The shape of the diagram is significant. The three-dimensional conical spiral is meant to suggest that, as we mature, we grow in capacity. We might not get taller anymore after our adolescent years, but we continue to grow emotionally. The engine for our growth is what Kegan calls the "subject-object relationship," depicted by the arrows in the diagram. When we are subject to an idea or influence, we are not aware of it. When we become aware of it, we find the capacity for objectivity and can consider different ways to approach that idea or influence. Kegan uses the example of the developmental shift from *being* someone's child, to that same child *having* parents. As the relationship shifts into objectivity, it matures.

The cone itself represents what Kegan and others call a "holding environment." Those who grow up in stable situations, with their basic needs met, are able to take the risks associated with growing and changing. Trauma disrupts the holding environment, as do broken promises from caregivers. Moving a concept in our minds from subject to object requires a certain trust that we are safe to take risks. Absent a holding environment, we are unlikely to trust enough to investigate our assumptions or our espoused values.

Kegan teaches that the left side of the diagram represents the extremes we experience in individuality—toddlerhood, young adulthood—and the right-side extremes of dependency—infancy (reliance on parents), adolescence (concern about the opinions of peers). Transitions between these stages can get messy sometimes. Consider the cooing infant who, seemingly overnight, becomes the stubborn toddler who loves the words "no" and "mine," and who insists on doing everything themselves. Or an adolescent who cares, or even becomes obsessed, about what their friends are doing; then, in an instant, they push away from everyone, baffling and worrying their support network as they attempt a fresh start on their own.

For the purposes of this book, the most important part of the diagram is at its very top: the most advanced stage, which I simply call "adulthood." Note how that stage is located at neither extreme of independence or interdependence. In adulthood, we find a way to manage both. What Rabbi Edwin Friedman would call the ideal leadership stance of "separate, yet connected,"[32] Kegan would simply call maturity. Mature persons accept that two different realities can be true at the same time, even in one person. An immature person—say, an interdependent teen, or a radically individualistic young adult—might consider a person for whom two things can be true at the same time a hypocrite. On the contrary, Kegan writes that adults need to be able to allow multiple truths to coexist within them simply to survive as a sane person.

Consider relationships with loved ones: we might not always like them. Are we to end relationships because we are annoyed or even appalled by the behaviors of those with whom we are connected? If so, we should expect an old age all alone. Consider the life of work: all jobs include duties we do not enjoy, even for those who are living fully into their callings. Do we quit at the first hint of a boring or overly arduous task? Do we walk off the job because we do not like our new boss or colleague? If so, we might bounce from job to job without ever making a deep impact.

For various reasons, many grow to be adults without ever entering "adulthood," if we define being grown-up as having the capacity to hold two or more truths simultaneously. One common and helpful example of arrested development comes as a result of alcoholism. One who starts drinking young as a way of coping with the challenges of relationships, anxiety, and responsibility might freeze themselves in Stage 3 above, "adolescence, dependence." One stuck in Stage 3 might remain throughout life entirely enmeshed with what others think. One mark of an alcoholic is black-and-white thinking, and such is the case for the immature as well. Some communities are specially designed to enable a person to remain at Stage 3. Some college's Greek organizations, for example, encourage groupthink and discourage individuation healthy for the young adult years, and they often use alcohol as the anesthesia that keeps pledges from adapting to a broader and more inclusive way of making sense of the world.

Some churches do the same. Here is the problem: Stage 3's outward signs include deep commitment to community. So does Stage 5, adulthood. Therefore, it is easy to mistake an immature person for a mature one in any context, and this is particularly unhealthy for churches. The most notable difference between such individuals is a subtle one: openness to change. A person in Stage 5 can think in terms of Beaumont's communitas. The church is more than a set of practices and has a transcendent identity in the mind of the mature person, so changes to practices are no threat. A person in Stage 3 cannot tell where they end and the congregation begins, and therefore, change presents an existential threat. When choosing a chair for a board, or a new staff member, or even a friend, all must take the time to discern whether the person they are considering is invested in a community because they need it— Stage 3—or because they are whole already but enriched by community—Stage 5. Then, they must choose the Stage 5 individual.

The next chapter will describe the five leadership tensions I propose can provide a framework in which to lead during an in-between and uncertain time. Built into the theory I will present is an important assumption: mature leaders can hold two values—even those at opposite extremes—at the same time, simultaneously and with integrity. Kegan presents us with evidence that healthy maturation includes growing capacity to hold the ironies of life in one meaning-making container and approach the oxymoronic riddles of human behavior with an open heart. To be a mature person in leadership helps, and what follows is a set of practices that allow leaders to enact their maturity in communal settings for which they hold some responsibility.

NOTES

31. Putnam and Campbell, *American Grace.*
32. Friedman, *A Failure of Nerve.*

PART TWO

Intentional Leadership

Whenever I hear the term "the cloud" in reference to technology, I feel a strange combination of exhilaration and dread. I can store endless amounts of data in the cloud. If my computer breaks, or is stolen, my data remain secure. Yet I cannot touch them, and I lack the expertise to navigate in the cloud except in a most elementary fashion. I mean the word "elementary" literally: most elementary school students know as much about the cloud as I do. Similarly, the image of leading in the cloud evokes both wonder at the possibilities and intimidation amidst unfamiliarity, which can feel scary to leaders who want and need to feel capable of carrying out their duties competently.

In a season of stability in an institution's life, the conventional leadership practices that provide a pattern for activity include casting a vision, setting goals, managing toward those goals, and evaluating effectiveness. In an in-between time, we must engage in all of these practices, in no small part because doing so instills confidence in the community that they are safe, and that everything is going to be alright. Yet the structure provided by those conventional practices is insufficient when it comes to energizing leaders and providing them with guidance as to where to point their attention.

The problem with conventional leadership practices lies in their linearity. A line is not wide enough to encompass the challenge of communal leadership in a complicated time that is characterized by internal diversity and external threats to togetherness. A line relies on a direction, and casting a singular direction in an uncertain time feels like a guessing game. Leaders must find a different image—a new theoretical framework—that accounts for both making progress and remaining present to the demands of liminality and all that for which the times call.

I propose that "tension" provides better guidance and motivation than "direction" when leading within a cloud of in-betweenness and uncertainty. In this section, I will describe five tensions that leaders can balance intentionally, or in-tension-ally. They help leaders know where to place their attention (a-tension?) when goals are not enough.

9

INDIVIDUALITY VERSUS COMMUNITY

The first tension carries implications both for the leader as an individual and for choosing the extent to which the leader is part of the community. Furthermore, this tension might provide guidance on when it is best to treat members of a community as part of a whole, and when to treat each individual as wholly separate, as both definitions of wholeness are worthy and true.

Leaders who go it alone are vulnerable to self-delusion, isolation, and burnout. In her article, "Leaving the Lone Ranger Mentality—Alone,"[33] Brenda A. Jenkins points out the importance of Jesus' friendships. She writes that the key to spiritual relationships between pastors and congregations is tending to the balance between the vertical and the horizontal: relating with the divine and relating with the community. Why do some leaders choose to go it alone, or only reach out for help rather than meaningful dialogue?

For most, arrogance is not the answer to that question, but rather insecurity. What if I connect deeply with another person, and that person sees my shortcomings and knows I am not just imperfect but deeply flawed? In other cases, leaders become Lone Rangers out of fear of criticism. Nobody likes criticism, and even if opening ourselves up to it might save pain down the line, we avoid encounters that might lead to our being criticized the same way we avoid prophylactic dental care. Finally, we might choose to lead individualistically because we fear not getting our own way if we open ourselves to the ways of others, forgetting sometimes that neither "our way" nor "their way" is God's way. Jenkins and others argue persuasively that clergy should connect meaningfully with colleagues for the sake of both support and reality-testing. Go with God and walk with colleagues; never go it alone.

In an article entitled "Toward a Theory of Spiritual Leadership,"[34] Louis Fry offers a different perspective on individuality in leadership. Fry makes a distinction between intrinsic and extrinsic motivation. Extrinsic motivation, namely our drive to please others or do their bidding, originates in fear. Leaders should not operate from it, nor should they tap into the fear of others to get them to follow. The spiritual leader stokes a community's *intrinsic* motivation to find meaning and satisfaction in life. It would be easy to jump to the conclusion that leaders who are flashy and charismatic bring out the *extrinsic* motivations of their communities, but not all charismatic leaders call on their communities to do their bidding. Interestingly, Fry suggests that charismatic leaders can be powerful intrinsic motivators for others if, and only if, they inspire in their communities a desire for a more meaningful life.

In my experience as a minister in the United Church of Christ, charismatic leadership gets a bad rap. Of course, charismatic leaders enjoy a certain amount of privilege, so sometimes we dislike them just because they remind us of people who abused their privilege or broke our trust. We might feel envy toward charismatic leaders—calling them "golden boys" and assuming they have not had to work as hard or suffer as long as we have—but concerns should run deeper than garden variety jealousy. Concerns about charismatic leaders might include:

- A slippery slope toward boundary violations. Charismatic leaders excite their followers and thus might cause those followers to lower their inhibitions, rendering them vulnerable to power abuses.

- A performative form of ministry in which the leader ministers from a false—appearance-obsessed—self and thus draws out that same tendency in adherents.

- A pattern of expectation in which successors to charismatic leaders are expected to titillate and evoke emotion the same way as their predecessors and are deemed failures when this does not happen.

As valid as these concerns are, I believe they only apply when a leader is charismatic and nothing else. If a leader is a stimulating and exciting preacher, for example, but lacks deep and abiding faith, then over time they become a hollow shell, and those who listen to them might model themselves after that same flawed form of piety. Conversely, an exciting and inspiring leader with great depth—of faith, of thought, of life experience, in relationships—inspires others to grow in every direction. To use Fry's language, a leader can be a powerful intrinsic motivator for good or for ill. Charisma is not the problem; in fact, leaders need it to motivate others to seek a more life-giving way of being in the world. The distinction comes when we consider what the charismatic leader does with that capacity to motivate: inspire people to put them on a higher pedestal, or inspire people to grow more fully into their callings from God? A charismatic leader can either draw all attention to themselves or use it to energize communal transformation.

The tension between individuality and community about which leaders must concern themselves, therefore, cuts in two directions. The leader must pay attention to how they cultivate individual members of their community, as well that community's togetherness and shared identity. Relatedly, the leader must consider their own identity as an individual while also fostering meaningful connections with colleagues and with the community, although those connections of course take different forms. The implications for practice emerging from this tension, individuality and community, are numerous and complex.

Leaders nurture individuals within the community as individuals, not just part of the whole. Balancing the wellbeing of individuals with the wellbeing of the whole community is one of leadership's classic challenges, and philosophers and theologians have struggled with it for centuries. That struggle plays out today as leaders seek to pay attention to the groups they lead, as well as individuals within the groups, with relative evenness.

I have spent much of my career in higher education, with my early working years spent advising college students in-residence. I learned in that work that, whereas college residential leaders rely heavily on mental health professionals in supporting students, mental health professionals do not always see dormitory life situations the same way a hall director might. For example, I once found myself in a dispute with a student's psychiatrist who wanted to discharge the student to his dormitory after that student shared with his roommates that he wanted to end his own life. The roommates—who were taking exams while also extremely worried about their friend—would keep an eye on him, thought the psychiatrist. I pled with the clinician to allow the student who was in crisis to stay in the infirmary for the sake of the community. The psychiatrist was, understandably, thinking primarily about the patient as an individual; my responsibility was different.

Another example of seeking the right balance between nurturing individuals in the community and attending to the needs of the community as a whole relates to lifting up leaders. In the United Church of Christ, leadership is shared among clergy, lay leaders, and the congregation's full membership. Clergy play an important role in developing lay leaders, providing them with spiritual guidance that helps them help the congregation as a whole to listen for God's call and thrive in living it out. The first step in leadership development is identification and recruitment of those with talent. Experienced ministers know that nurturing and lifting up mature and gifted lay leaders is absolutely key to the community's overall health.

As described in the last chapter, identifying who might be a healthy and mature potential leader requires careful attention. Consider Kegan's expanding spiral and remember: the outward comportment of a radically interconnected and immature adolescent, and a whole-yet-connected seasoned adult, might look very similar. Both seek relationships and often present themselves for leadership roles. The pastor or executive leader must work to tell the difference between the immature and the mature, and then recruit the mature into leadership. Does this mean playing favorites? Some might think so, but when the health of the organization is at stake, the executive sometimes must risk being perceived as privileging some over others if doing so leads to recruitment of suitable lay leaders.

Put differently, multiple options exist for nurturing individuals within a community; advancing people into leadership is just one, and for many it is not the best one. Giving out promotions is not a good way to say, "I see and care about you." The best way to say that is to... say that. One way leaders can pay attention to nurturing individuals in the communities they serve is by keeping a prayer list and taking time each day to reach out, simply and briefly, to those on it. Paying careful attention to staff evaluation schedules so that those who serve do not feel like their careers are ignored; replying to every email, even with just the words "got it"—these small gestures ensure that individuals do not feel like they have been agglomerated into a whole but are known as wholly human.

Sometimes, when leaders are overwhelmed and tired, they begin doing just that: agglomerating. Our brains find a certain efficiency in seeing a community not as a group of individuals, but just as a group. We might fight that shortcut to be a time- and energy-saver, but those we lead can tell when we do not see them as separate and sacred. Do we therefore promote everyone—even the unqualified and immature—into leadership? No. Do we burn ourselves out attending to every last person at every moment? No. But we pay attention to both individuals in the community and the whole of the community with relative balance, at the rate our energy can allow.

In the cult classic film *Harold and Maude*, a love story about a young man and a much older and wiser woman, Maude—a Holocaust survivor—teaches Harold about joy and meaningful living. In one dialogue, Maude asks Harold what kind of flower he would be, were he a flower. Harold looks to the meadow before them to a swath of seemingly identical flowers and says he would probably be one of those. Maude carefully picks one of the flowers and chastises Harold for dismissing its specialness by lumping it in with all the others. She points to its unique characteristics and imperfections and then muses that many of the world's problems result from a failure to see the worth of each and every created thing for having only seen the group as a whole.

Perceiving individuals first as parts of a group, and only secondarily as whole and valuable in and of themselves, can result in dismissal of their humanity. Maude, having survived a concentration camp, knew too well what it meant to be categorized and dismissed. The human tendency to take mental shortcuts and impose labels is to be resisted. We resist through our intentionality, balancing attention to individuals and attention to the group.

Failure to pay attention results in a high cost: if we allow our instincts to take over, they will lead us in unhealthy directions. We might overlook individuals as we attempt to focus on the community, alienating people, or stereotyping them, or oppressing them. Conversely, we might become overly concerned about individuals, finding ourselves swayed by the loudest, angriest, or most vocal individuals, not realizing that they are not representative of the community. We might trick ourselves into thinking that we have to approach everyone exactly the same way in order not to be hypocrites. When overwhelmed, we might lump people together as a shortcut because the fact that all are different from one another can be overwhelming. Just like walking on a balance beam takes strength and energy, so does intentional leadership that attends to communities as well as individuals.

Leaders care for themselves as individuals while also nesting themselves in a community of colleagues. My colleague-now-friend Kathy taught me most of what I know about teamwork. When I first joined the faculty at Andover Newton as director of field education and tenure-track professor of ministerial leadership, Kathy was the Field Education Program's associate director and had been in the acting role the year before I came. She valued working closely together. I thought I did too, but I really had not had enough experience on healthy teams to know how much they could change a person. Previous to that role, I had been part of unhealthy teams and of no team. I knew only in theory how much better people could help one another to become through collaboration. I still communicate with Kathy several times each week and think about her even more often. We started a conversation in 2005 that is still unfolding.

It might then surprise you to hear that when Kathy went on sabbatical, I found the job much easier without her. She and I reflected on this when she returned. Not having to run ideas by other people made for smoother days and faster work. I told Kathy, "The job is easier alone, but I'm much better at it when you are here." The resistance colleagues present forces us to be thoughtful. When we are in relationship with others who are familiar with the demands of our work, we hold ourselves accountable to ourselves and to them. We get outside ourselves to look in, and only then can we see what is really happening inside of us. Colleagues slow us down, maybe not in a way that we could measure with a clock, but in a way that forces us to be honest about what we are doing and why.

Leaders must attend to the community of colleagues around them. Those who are quick to ask for advice and feedback are less likely to make rash and unhelpful decisions; in other words, if we are going to be quick somewhere, we ought to be quick to get input so we might avoid careless mistakes. Leaders avoid opening themselves up to colleagues for a variety of reasons. They might be afraid to allow others to see their vulnerability and perhaps take advantage of it. They might want to rush through unpleasant feelings of not knowing what to do. They might not have learned how helpful colleagues can be, not having had good relationships with them previously, or having had role models who were Lone Rangers.

Whether they are constitutionally predisposed to introverted privacy or outgoing openness, today's leaders simply cannot get away with acting as Lone Rangers. Because the communities they lead are, by virtue of the changing times, increasingly diverse and complicated, they must connect with colleagues and friends in order to remain attuned to the way in which they are taking up space in the world. Only the trust we can find in admired colleagues and true friends can cause us to feel open enough to hear when we have gone in the wrong direction. We need to hear that truth and hear it in love. Leaders must form those bonds of trusting relationships when times are relatively calm, usually the very early days of a leadership role. The trust must grow during the good times so that, in the bad times, they feel known well enough to let their guards down. The first thing they should do when crisis is upon them is reach out to their support networks and put them on high alert.

My friend Amy is one of the people I truly trust. We have been friends and colleagues for more than twenty years. One of my earliest recollections of Amy's support for my ministry was through her reflective practice. When we had known each other for just a year or two, she described a tough meeting that she had taken part in and asked, "What do you think I might have been contributing to the dynamic?" I was surprised, yet moved, by the question. Usually, I leaned on friends to tell me, "Sarah, you were right! They were wrong! You are perfect!" I certainly expect that of my spouse, Dan! Amy showed me that she trusted me enough to let her guard all the way down and learn from what she was right to expect to be my loving and nonjudgmental perspective.

Even though leaders need trusted confidants and can no longer function as Lone Rangers (if they ever could), they also must retain their own sense of identity. Recalling Kegan's spiral, the mature leader must be wholly able to hear and nondefensively respond to the thoughts of other people, while also having a position that is wholly their own. Sometimes, leaders must make choices that even their closest colleagues think are the wrong ones. They have more information about what is best for them and their communities than even their best friends could know. They also know better than others could what risks they are willing to tolerate, and which ones they are not. I remember one time seeking out a counselor during a difficult time in my professional life. At the beginning of the very first meeting, I shared that leaving my job was not an option; there were important professional and personal reasons this was so. I shared that I needed to trust she understood that the option of quitting was off the table if I was to build trust. She agreed, and we proceeded.

In his final book, assembled after his death by his children, Rabbi Edwin Friedman[35] writes that the consummate leader is wholly distinct as a person and wholly connected with the community. Separate-yet-togetherness is the goal for the self-differentiated leader within an emotional system. This first tension of this book expands that idea to include not just the leader themselves but the leader's hopes and intentions toward the community. Leaders want all members of a community to be whole as well as integrated. Leaders cannot treat individuals as though they were some kind of collective intelligence and expect people to feel like they are seen and taken seriously. They also cannot treat each individual as an island unto themselves, both because of bandwidth issues and because doing so sends the wrong message about the nature of human community. The leader's daily mantra thus must be, "I am separate yet connected; those I lead are, too; how can I cultivate both of these dimensions in those I serve, and in myself, today?"

Due to the Covid-19 pandemic, the university that my seminary is embedded in changed the academic calendar for 2020–2021 during the summer before the first semester began. Leaders wisely chose to expand the mid-semester break and virtually eliminate days off during the semester, hoping to minimize students' temptation to travel away and bring the novel coronavirus back to campus with them. One of the several negative, unintended consequences of this necessary adaptation was that students who relied on campus jobs to pay their bills were left high-and-dry in January.

Each unit at Yale Divinity School, including Andover Newton Seminary, got to work creating opportunities for students to make up for lost wages through special projects. My staff colleagues and I created an initiative we called The Andover NewDeal. We employed any and all students in our program who wished to work during the month of January. Initially, we expected three to five students; ultimately, we employed twenty-two in five different teams that functioned incredibly creatively, inspiringly.

In the midst of the Andover NewDeal, on a particularly busy day of supervision and coordination, our campus minister dropped me a note that a student not participating in the program had offhandedly mentioned he was planning to take the spring semester off. This course of action is unusual in our community; unplanned semesters away sometimes spell crises in health or changes in callings. A few days later, that news sunk in for me. Why did it take so long for me to react to the news? Because I was so focused on community-wide thinking that I had lost track of an individual. I reached out to the student to set up a time to talk as soon as the realization came upon me that I lead not just a community, but a community of individual human beings.

It was important for me to go easy on myself at that moment, and in the many moments before and since when I have had to change my focus. And "focus" is perhaps the best action verb available for sustaining the tension between community and individuality. My colleague Kathryn Windsor, with whom I directed the field education program at Andover Newton Theological School, liked to use the metaphor of a photograph's foreground and background. When composing a photograph, the photographer points the lens toward what they want to capture, and that which is in the background becomes blurrier. The photographer might move the lens, however, pointing it at something in the background and causing the foreground to blur. Similarly, in leadership, we often move our attention, but what might have been happening in our blurrier line of vision is important, and we should not miss it.

Leaders must develop habits and disciplines that make shifting from community to individual and back again possible. One of my ministry role models, the Rev. Rick Huleatt, keeps a careful pastoral record. On the anniversary of a funeral, he will reach out to the family to see how they are. He gifted me with a pastoral record book when I was ordained, and I have in turn gifted others with the same. Rick also manages boards and systems with expertise. That capacity to shift attention from macro to micro requires a system, and we need the same to ensure that we shift our focus regularly, irrespective of what is shouting most loudly for our attention.

The Covid-19 pandemic has placed a strain on many leaders' capacities to sustain this tension. I can only speak with authority on the effect it has had on me: I spend much more time alone, so I know my own mind because of all the time it and I spend together. I must rely on written words (email) and pictures on a screen (Zoom) to ascertain how our community is doing. Whereas I would typically get whipped up into the community's mood during a crisis, the crises that have come and gone during Covid-19, and the crisis of the pandemic itself, have hit me quite differently. I have a certain distance from crises, which one would think would give me the capacity to reflect on them, but my reflection partners are miles away. I am just as likely to perseverate on that which I cannot control, so I must keep a healthy psychological distance, which might seem counterintuitive given that "distance" is one thing we have in abundance.

More obvious is the fact that I have to work hard to stay connected with people. I am quicker to pick up the phone rather than sending an email, quicker to say "let's meet over Zoom" than talk on the phone. Still, misunderstandings and hurt feelings crop up in the most surprising places due to the loss of intuition that comes from physical separation. My capacity to read a room in-person does not carry over to Zoom rooms; I have to ask a lot of questions about how people are doing and what they are thinking in Zoom meetings. At the same time, obsessing about how others are feeling and thinking distracts me from my own leadership agenda, which is not good for my institution. The necessity of paying attention to my individual identity and my connectivity with the community has become even more urgent, and becoming disconnected from one or the other seems a clear and present danger.

NOTES

33. Brenda A. Jenkins, "Leaving the Lone Ranger Mentality—Alone," in *African American Church Leadership: Principles for Effective Ministry and Community Leadership*, ed. Lee N. June and Christopher C. Mathis, Jr. (Grand Rapids, MI: Kregel Ministry, 2013), 175–92.

34. Fry, "Toward a Theory of Spiritual Leadership."

35. Friedman, *A Failure of Nerve.*

10

INCLUSIVITY VERSUS CLEAR IDENTITY

The second leadership tension this book promotes as one worthy of careful consideration is that of inclusivity (hospitality and abundant welcome) and clear identity (special set-apartness). All of us want to feel like we belong, but the nature of belonging is rife with internal contradictions. We feel like we belong when we are welcomed warmly and included fully by virtue of who we really are. The immediate problem that emerges from that feeling of belonging is the nature of scarcity. We cannot believe that a community could have the capacity to welcome everyone as fully as it welcomes us. The child within us wants to feel like we are getting special treatment, not the same another might encounter. A greeting we receive that is available to anyone at all is not as meaningful as feeling singled out as a unique individual. Finding the right balance between opening our arms and causing those to whom we have opened those arms to feel important requires intentional leadership.

More than ten years ago, I partnered with colleagues to study the practices of a UCC congregation that was having notable success in attracting members who were in their twenties. The church was traditional: organ music rather than a band, committees and coffee hour, and no special outreach to younger adults that might explain growth in that demographic. Around the time our study began, a new member Sunday included thirty joining the church, twenty-seven of whom were under thirty years of age. Given how many churches were failing to connect with younger adults, I and others were curious and investigated what might account for the phenomenon.

One of the many reasons younger adults felt drawn to the church was that they received hospitality that did not feel needy or make them uncomfortable. When they visited the church, young adults witnessed members seeming truly happy to be in church, and also truly happy to see and welcome them, but with no veiled expectations. Young adults described experiences of visiting small and struggling churches and feeling as though they were beset by insecure members who desperately craved a sign that the church could grow. Remembering Kegan's spiral, we know that younger adults seek identity through individuality; neediness is the ultimate turnoff.

Perhaps the clearest example we can find of a balance between inclusivity and clear identity is in immigrant faith communities. In *American Grace*,[36] sociologists Robert Putnam and David Campbell write about the way in which some immigrant groups assimilate to the United States in every way except religion. Immigrants often become part of churches that give them a place to hold onto the culture of their countries of origin, sustaining their ethnic identities through religion while they seek an assimilative inclusion outside the church. They find in immigrant churches welcome and inclusion for a particular part of themselves.

Putnam and Campbell consider predominately Black churches as "the quintessential example of a fusion between ethnicity and religion."[37] Whereas many white, liberal Americans (like me) crave multiethnic religious experience and feel ambivalent about worshiping in an all-white congregation, Black Christian churches play an important identity formation role for some Black Americans. Those who spend significant parts of their week in settings where they are in the minority need a break from working to be and feel included. They need a place where they can allow their identities room to breathe.

Out of all the tensions described in this book, I believe the necessity that leaders both cultivate a warm welcome while also causing their communities to feel special and set apart is the most difficult, and it is also the tension that is changing most quickly. I believe that the high degree of difficulty associated with sustaining this tension results from cultural change that requires and deserves some explanation. In Chapter 2, I wrote about the cultural movement from the modern era to the postmodern era and now into the era some are calling that of new tribalism. This successive flow from era to era figures prominently in the balance leaders must strike between inclusivity and strong identity. We must take a moment to consider the role of changing cultural eras as we explore changing demands upon communal leaders.

To review, in the United States and Western Europe, intellectual historians describe the "modern era" as the season that spanned from the nineteenth through the mid-twentieth centuries. Technological innovation and the belief that human beings could achieve virtually anything characterized the era. A Christian worldview dominated, but scientific ways of viewing the world also blended into frameworks for meaning-making, and more culturally influential branches of the Christian movement collaborated willingly with science's reshaping of thought. Those with power were of European descent, male, straight, cisgender, able-bodied, and Protestant—and then, there was everyone else.

The 1960s and early 1970s marked a time of cultural shift away from the rule-bound, Truth-with-a-capital-T, humanistic, modern era. A combination of those holding the power making a mess of the world, and those without power finding their voices, led to a time of unrest and dramatic change, both to the good and the ill. To the good, some who had been previously excluded from the corridors of power found their places at the table, as subject to regression as that progress might seem. To the ill, institutions that held communities together began to struggle and fail. Of course, institutions have a lot to answer for; that said, when they fail, something new needs to rise up in their places if people are going to build a society together.

The postmodern era, characterized by a no-rules and no-single-definition-of-truth outlook on the world, seems to have begun to crumble by the early 2010s. Technology began to make it possible for people to coalesce again around shared interests without the brick-and-mortar institutions that made doing so possible previously. Some call the dawning era a time of "new tribalism." A tribe, in this case, would be a small unit of those with shared interests protecting and supporting each other. The difference between the tribalism of the past that relied on geographical proximity and today is that we can become parts of far-flung tribes, and many of them.

Leaders are just beginning to understand the implications of new tribalism for building community, and this is where finding and maintaining tension between inclusivity and clear identity comes in. People want to feel welcomed and respond warmly to hospitality. They also want to feel like they are part of something through which they can self-actualize, expressing their identities through their various memberships. Therefore, if the entire identity of a community is "all are welcome," it lacks the specificity needed to cause a person to feel like they are making a statement by becoming part of it.

In the United Church of Christ, radical welcome is not just a practice but part of our identity. People come to the United Church of Christ because they seek a Christian community that does not exclude those whose identities do not fit outdated norms for what a Christian looks like, loves like, is like. That said, many worry that the denomination does a better job describing its inclusivity than its clear identity. As for the latter—as an old saying about boring worship goes—people come hungry and leave starving. People come to the UCC because they want inclusivity and object morally to exclusivity. What, then, makes them stay?

The leadership advice I want to impart about sustaining the tension between inclusivity and clear identity is this: cultivate hospitality in the general atmosphere and then work like crazy to build community among those who gather. Only through opportunities to form bonds among the likeminded can a person grateful to have been included come to feel like they belong. There was once a time in my life when I thought religious organizations should stay away from fellowship that was not specifically religious—perhaps in my own Kegan Stage 4 of radical individualism, perhaps in the thick of postmodernity—but I have come to understand that people need "their people" in this era. If they do not find it in a healthy, life-giving, and loving setting, they will look for it someplace else.

And there are plenty of negative arenas in which people find "their people." Consider those who occupy demographic categories that used to, and often still do, receive certain privileges: white, straight, cisgender men. Technology makes it possible for such people to find each other, feast on anger, cultivate resentment toward those who now share privileged spaces with them, and form a mental model for scapegoating. Frightening as it is to imagine, white supremacist groups give those who join them a sense of specialness they feel they deserve and have lost. Wanting to feel special is no crime; our society needs healthier ways to offer that specialness.

To feed the need for specialness and community, while also resisting the tendency groups sometimes demonstrate to set up a "you and me against the world" mentality around belonging, is a form of peacemaking. When we learn of a young person who has been radicalized online by a terrorist organization, of course we want to punish both the organization and the young person. We must also ask the question: what was that group providing that young person that they could not find in a healthier way? Those who work with urban youth have long understood that gangs provide a sense of communal support sadly lacking elsewhere. We can either dedicate resources to incarcerating gang members who commit crimes, or we can create structures of communal support, but in reality some thoughtful combination will be necessary to effect change.

During the postmodern era, attempts at inclusivity at times took away cherished settings of community in the name of equality. In his memoir *Colored People*,[38] Henry Louis Gates, Jr. writes about the joy and togetherness he experienced in segregated events in his hometown in West Virginia, and the loss to the community caused by the eradication of such events. As mentioned previously, Putnam and Campbell write in *American Grace*[39] about the way in which immigrants seek out pockets of belonging so they might find respite regularly from pressure to assimilate, refueling their cultural identities and finding support and encouragement.

The newly tribal era has the capacity to offer something different from postmodernity's chronic isolation. We are entering a cultural moment of both/and, where people are able to participate in society as a whole, while also finding niches of belonging that give them rest from the chaos of day-to-day living. Consider the 2020 presidential election: voter turnout was astonishingly high as compared with previous elections, even amidst a pandemic, which tells us that Americans have a sense of being part of something bigger than their local communities. At the same time, different subgroups interpreted everything about the election—even the very question of who won it—differently from one another.

I believe this moment of transition between the postmodern era and a newly tribal era holds tremendous potential for churches if they can recognize how they must reach out differently now than they have in the past. In the modern era, people went to church and attended to other civic duties (and notice how religion was among their civic, rather than the spiritual, duties) as a matter of cultural expectation. During the postmodern era, when "duty" became a four-letter word for many, churches never managed to adjust fully. They relied on vestigial senses of responsibility innate to those raised during the modern era, expecting a homing beacon to kick in, which it did, but with less intensity with each generation. The churches that were able to survive and thrive found a way to tap into something more than duty. They connected with people emotionally, helped people to find and tend a sense of spirituality, and then they found ways to get people to connect with each other.

Religion in a diverse society has the potential to serve as a life-giving kind of tribe, but it must adjust to the notion that people will be part of many different tribes during their lifetimes. Faith can help people to create a cohesive set of communities in their lives. What does it mean to maintain a healthy relationship with numerous tribes? Consider the cells in a human body. Healthy cells have semi-permeable membranes. Oxygen can get in, and carbon dioxide can get out. Nutrients can get in, and waste can get out. But the membrane has integrity, too. It is because of the membrane that cells can be connected to each other and yet separate, serving their own function. A cell whose membrane has deteriorated is a cell that is dying or dead.

Similarly, faith communities are surrounded by membranes, or what theologian Gabriel Fackre called a perimeter.[40] Even the United Church of Christ, which places welcome and acceptance of all at the center of its values, must have a perimeter around it that contains that for which it stands and keeps separate that which it does not embrace. Inside the perimeter, a clear identity is crucial to the tradition's integrity. Prospective members will want to know it, and those within the perimeter will not feel special without it. Putnam and Campbell write that, in American religion, most people come for the theology and stay for the friendships. If the church's theology is impossible to ascertain, as the community is bending over backwards to welcome everyone, newcomers will feel uncomfortable and confused, like someone is trying to sell them something without telling them what it is. Churches today must figure out how they are going to situate themselves in the newly tribal reality, where overt statements about identity are necessary in addition to atmospheres of welcome and hospitality.

First Church in Cambridge struck a balance that young adults found attractive: a healthy tension between being open to all and having strong convictions. One might assume that the best way to make new young adults feel welcome in a church would be to say to them, "Whatever you want us to be, we will be that." Instead, FCC embodied one of the customary greetings of the United Church of Christ: "Whoever you are, and wherever you are on life's journey, you are welcome here." FCC has a theology, and a clear and strong one at that: it is a generously welcoming Christian church. Young adults in an era of new tribalism crave a sense of ideological belonging, and if that ideology is mushy, they will feel anxious.

United Church of Christ theologian Gabriel Fackre wrote that a tradition must have a perimeter that delineates where it ends and other traditions begin.[41] The UCC is proud of its openness, and, ironically, its openness creates a perimeter: we are not like other traditions that expect ideological uniformity. Leaders must take care to describe the nature of this openness—its theological roots—and avoid the temptation to over-promise. Perhaps this leadership practice sounds easy, but it is not. Disappointing those who want to stretch the perimeter beyond an organization's mission or philosophy can be difficult, especially in institutions where hierarchies are flat, which leaves questions about who has the authority to define the community's identity.

Striking the right balance between inclusivity ("all are welcome") and strong identity ("we stand for something") is more art than science. Welcome and hospitality are values that, when embraced, mean new ideas flow into an organization. As those ideas interact catalytically with an existing mission and identity, the nature of the organization changes at a cellular level by virtue of the newness introduced. The leader who attempts to squelch that interaction and reaction, or the community that makes no room for new ideas, soon finds itself stuck.

Even worse, the community that seeks to prevent catalytic change introduced by new people and ideas renders meaningless any hospitality it attempted to extend. To welcome a person only insofar as they are willing to conform is not to welcome a person at all. Therefore, if inclusivity is to be true rather than false, the community's identity must be both strong and supple. The perimeter around it must be like a cell in an organism: semi-permeable to let in that which is life-giving, cast out that which is death-dealing, and change without the membrane becoming unhealthy and disintegrating.

Much is yet to be discovered regarding the appropriate balance between building strong tribes and critiquing the effects they have on wider society. Building relationships with those who share our values and priorities is healthy and life-giving. We need the support that comes with choosing relationships with those we respect and admire. Yet, conversely, when people limit the voices they hear to those with which they agree, they lose capacity to share spaces with those who are different from them, as they get out of practice with feeling the discomfort natural to human interactions beyond ourselves.

One helpful framing for striking the appropriate balance between the all-are-welcome inclusivity of a community and cultivation of its special distinctiveness comes to us from secondary education. John Palfrey wrote an essay entitled *Safe Spaces, Brave Spaces: Diversity and Free Expression in Education*[42] while serving as the head of an independent, residential, secondary school. He argues that young people require two types of settings for formation: some where they experience radical acceptance, and some where they feel challenged to express themselves without reassurances that they will be understood or affirmed. Of course, a perfect balance cannot be struck. For example, those who come from demographic groups who have long occupied corridors of power (wealthy, white, male, able-bodied, cisgender, straight, etc.) will find that most spaces feel safe. Others who come from minoritized groups might find that most spaces require their bravery. Still, the goal of striving to accomplish a mixture of safe and brave spaces for an educational community seems a worthy one when considering the human need for unconditional acceptance in community, alongside the human tendency to stop growing when too often occupying settings where our views go unchallenged.

Again, in an era of new tribalism, a sense of belonging requires not just one-on-one friendships but a sense of alignment with communal identity. Whereas, in a postmodern cultural soup, downplaying strong convictions might have been good for business, today's new tribalism resists vague stances; they are unattractive and untrusted. The college that says "we're right for everyone" comes across as right for no one. The private club that says "anything goes" does not cause those who are part of it to feel special. And people want to feel welcome, but they also want to feel special, and the perfect balance between the two is not down the middle. Leaders must cultivate openness and welcome while also continuously clarifying the organization's identity through defining mission, articulating values, and distinguishing what makes it unique and essential. Leaders must attend to both ends of the spectrum between inclusivity and clear identity, cultivating missional clarity and opening doors wide, in repeating and regular sequence.

Today's leaders must consciously create a life-giving community with a strong sense of belonging, held together by the connective tissue of relationships among individuals, in order to feed the need for a tribe that has a clear identity and shared values. The hope is that healthy tribes will have a catalytic effect on the whole society. They present an option for finding a sense of belonging that is creative rather than destructive with salutary effects on the wider society's wellbeing. Put simply, a person who has a healthy sense of belonging in one setting—within one cellular membrane—can bring that sense to another, and those in that setting could bring that sense to yet more, different tribes. The goal of creating a sense of belonging is not to eradicate divisions, but to teach people how to be whole and yet connected.

NOTES

36. Putnam and Campbell, *American Grace*.

37. Ibid., 264.

38. Henry Louis Gates, Jr., *Colored People: A Memoir*, 1st ed. (New York: Knopf, 1994).

39. Putnam and Campbell, *American Grace*.

40. Gabriel J. Fackre, *Believing, Caring, and Doing in the United Church of Christ: An Interpretation* (Cleveland: United Church Press, 2005).

41. Ibid.

42. John G. Palfrey, *Safe Spaces, Brave Spaces: Diversity and Free Expression in Education* (Cambridge, MA: The MIT Press, 2017).

11

PLANNING VERSUS NIMBLENESS

During the pandemic, I planned a birthday celebration on Zoom for a friend. My friend's birthday is close to Christmas, so it often goes unnoticed, and this year, the pandemic would make it impossible to take her out on the town. I told my friend I wanted to do this, and that I was hoping to work with her young adult daughter, whom I have come to love through the transitive property: I love my friend, and my friend adores her daughter who lives in another city, far away. My friend's daughter and I threw together a party in record time and had much fun and laughter together in the process.

The night of the event, I was the behind-the-scenes stage manager, and my friend's daughter served as the emcee. We had a solid plan for how the hour would be spent, but from the very start, a guest with the best of intentions took the order of events in an unexpected direction, rushing ahead to a later part of the program. Those attending the party on Zoom saw the cohosts smiling and nodding and delighting. If they could have seen the chat function in Zoom between the cohosts, they would have seen a different story. My friend's daughter and I rapidly, though not frantically, rethought the order for the hour and adjusted to the flow. We could have grabbed the reins and rerouted the party audibly, but doing so would have changed a warm atmosphere into a rigid one. In order to let go of our initial plan, however, we could not just "go with the flow." We needed to consciously rethink what to let go and what not to.

Oliver Wendell Holmes, Sr. famously stated, "For the simplicity on this side of complexity, I wouldn't give you a fig. But for the simplicity on the other side of complexity, for that I would give you anything I have." Another way of expressing Holmes's hope would be to say that simplicity is beautiful, but one has to do the work. Going with the flow is the same way. There is nimbleness that comes as a result of preparation for any possible contingencies, and there is nimbleness that results from having no plan at all. Anyone who has read my writing about planning and evaluation would of course expect that I hold planning in high regard. I also am learning more and more about how lovely and wonderful nimbleness can be when coupled with thoughtfulness as opposed to indifference.

One of the reasons I value planning—and its counterpart, evaluation—so greatly is because I believe planning tells a community that its leaders care. For that reason, planning that becomes so airtight and inflexible that members of the community cannot express their own hopes and feelings runs counter to what makes planning meaningful. The planning that silences voices is paternalism, condescension, autocracy. The ideal, therefore, is a simple but thought-out plan, developed inclusively and nimble enough to bend without breaking. How can leaders find that right tension between having clear plans, and wisdom to know when to set those plans aside? What follows are two different leadership approaches that give us models for considering this tension.

In an article entitled "Pastoral Leadership as a Dance: How Embodiment, Practice and Identity Shape Communities and their Leadership,"[43] Belgium-based theologian Jack Barentsen describes the interpretive motions of pastoral leadership—both physical and dialogical—as movement enacting the music of life flowing around us. Barentsen debunks the classical "Great Man Theory" of leadership so prevalent in Western thought, where we tell aspiring leaders that the path toward greatness is to study the paths of famous and powerful others. He instead argues that leadership is more art than science, and therefore, leadership development results from learning how to listen to the music and respond from the heart.

"Dancing ... can be defined as the continuous and emotion-filled embodied interaction between dance partners, in a sequence of both studied and spontaneous moves,"[44] writes Barentsen. Good dancers are both highly trained and emotionally present, interpreting what happens inside them, in response to a context, through movement. Leadership is much the same way: training and presence lead to both preparation and flexibility. Considering leadership as an art provides us with a powerful new perspective on its nature. In leadership, as in dance, we move into and out of ritualized practices.

When leading an institution, authorized leaders move between and through conversations, events, and meetings. As with any ritual, the participants have expectations based on previous experience, some explicit and some implicit. A leader needs to honor those expectations while clearly communicating their own. Showing up—being present physically—sends a strong message about our priorities. When we arrive a few minutes early, prepared and ready to be of service, we signal that an engagement is important. When we arrive late or not at all, or we are only physically but not emotionally present, we say that an event is not important to us. Leaders also carry a responsibility to make a meeting or event worthwhile and engaging. If we use a leader's convening power to bring people together, but then do not take full advantage of their time and wisdom, we fail in our responsibility to be good dance partners; we fail in our responsibility to provide a strong and guiding frame for the energies of those we asked to show up and who did so out of respect for our authority.

To show up fully in one's leadership setting requires prior planning. One has to have put aside other concerns, organizing competing commitments in such a way that they do not intrude. Then, when in the leadership context, one has to exert effort to read the situations one encounters, including both what was planned and what came up over the transom. Susan Beaumont calls this "presence," which is not the opposite of planning. The two overlap in a quantum mechanical way, coexisting on two different planes of reality, which requires us to blend the two based on the circumstances we encounter.

A spouse of a colleague works in corporate law with a focus on technology. The spouse is female in a male-dominated profession, but she does not choose to engage coworkers about sexism. When she experiences sexist stereotypes through the words she hears or choices made, she simply, literally, walks out. In a board meeting, in a conversation with a team member, she will get up and walk away. I am not sure how I could ever carry out such a bold form of resistance given my context, but the dance of absenting ourselves exhibits the way in which we can use nimbleness as activism. Our body says, "I am not going to adjust to your disrespect."

There is, indeed, a certain line between being nimble and being a doormat. I sometimes get feedback that I was overly rigid about agendas, yet I also receive high praise for all that gets accomplished when groups I lead stay on task. I find that male participants on teams I lead are much more likely to push back—usually through making fun of me for my "controlling" ways—on the plans I present, even when they have agreed to those plans. When I hold them accountable to their own agreements, and they chafe, who is the rigid one in that interchange? As you can see, planning and nimbleness are not as simple as one might expect, but rather fraught with power dynamics, creative possibilities, and the need for leaders who are mature and self-differentiated.

An immature person needs a plan in order to stay focused and not become overly fused with a community, but the immature person cannot set a plan aside when doing so is for the best. They have difficulty sustaining two truths (such as, "this plan is great; but it is no longer serving us") at the same time. How do I know this? Because I myself have gone through a journey of this type, moving from *needing* a plan to knowing all goes better with a plan. I once preached from manuscripts where I selected every word with care; now I usually use an outline. I used to get bent out of shape when plans changed, and now I might sense mild irritation but will not sacrifice the quality of an event for worship of my beloved plan. The shift has been subtle over twenty-five years of ministry, but when I look at old documents and manuscripts, I both cringe at how controlling I imagine I seemed and smile that I now see the other side of complexity.

Between planning and nimbleness, each of us has a default mode where we feel most comfortable. Some of us are planners who have learned nimbleness; others naturally go with the flow but have learned the importance of planning. Leaders who can function at the intersection of planning and nimbleness are the leaders best situated to succeed in an in-between era that is replete with unprecedented challenges.

Andover Newton's board of trustees is the finest board I have ever known. Our chair is a consultant who helps boards improve, so she brings expertise to the design of all we do together. We meet three times each year in person, with Zoom meetings in between so that the group does not grow too distanced from the goings-on of our seminary. The in-person board meetings require a great deal of advance planning, as all committees and staff report on progress toward accomplishing our mission. We have guest speakers who are usually students, but sometimes visitors like the dean of the divinity school where we are embedded, Yale Divinity School. As I write, one of our three in-person meetings of the year is coming up tomorrow, although we will be on Zoom due to the pandemic. All is ready to plug-and-play.

Or, I should say, all *was* ready. Last night, I received an email from the YDS dean asking that our board consider making an important move now, rather than waiting for a future date as had been our previous intention. What he asked us to consider is not important to this chapter. What is important is the stress I felt when reading his email, and as I mulled the request over in my mind. We have such a pretty little meeting organized for tomorrow! Every detail in place! But the request was urgent, time-sensitive, and important.

Were I not reluctant to let go of my illusion of control, and my delight in thinking a plan was both complete and watertight, I would think nothing of asking our board chair to change our agenda to discuss and decide on the YDS dean's matter of concern. Ultimately, I expect I will do something like using the time set aside for my report to the board to lay out the request, and then ask for a special meeting in a week or two to discuss the proposal in-depth after I have done some due diligence, and after the board has a chance to think about the situation. I will not ask that we alter the board meeting's essential structure, but I will use the flexibility built into the agenda to tee up the topic for another day in the near future.

Cultivating the right tension between planning and nimbleness enables leaders to move ahead toward their goals and their institutions' visions while maintaining readiness for whatever comes in over the transom. I learned the expression, "Whatever comes in over the transom," while serving on a search committee several years ago. A member of the committee insisted on asking every candidate about how they handled a totally unexpected crisis. She felt that the best way to get to know a leaders' style was to find out how they adjusted. A transom is a window over a door. If floodwater is so high it comes in over the transom, business-as-usual must come to an end. Leaders should not feel pressed to adjust to every knock on the door, but sometimes that which is on the other side of the door demands our attention.

For a truly skilled leader, plans and unexpected turns of events form a dialectical relationship with one another. The best way I know to define "dialectical" is to describe a conversation between two strangers. The first stranger tells their story, and by telling the story, they experience some catharsis and change. The hearer also changes by hearing the account. When the second stranger shares their story, they change for the telling, and the other stranger changes for the hearing. Conversations *change* people; they are not merely ex-changes of information. Similarly, planning and nimbleness are not two counterforces between which leaders ping-pong. Making a plan shapes the inner life of the leader, and unexpected twists and turns affect the plan. Both making the plan and responding to the unexpected constitute the leader's formation and continuing education on the job.

Nimbleness is not the same as reactivity. Having a plan and then blowing it up because circumstances change is usually a rookie leadership mistake. A healthy tension between planning and nimbleness means that we will not ignore crises or new information; at the same time, we will not be easily derailed. We will listen to crises for what they demand of us and what they try to teach us. We will pause and consider crises' urgency and formulate a mini plan-within-the-plan for addressing them. The mini plan will, of course, have a catalytic effect on the wider plan, like a grain of salt dissolving in water, changing the nature of the water. It does not, however, need to fundamentally upend the plan, unless the plan is one that deserves upending.

Today's civic society undervalues planning. We are currently in the midst of a crisis that has taken hundreds of thousands of lives, which resulted in part from poor planning. The Obama administration created a pandemic playbook that included what would have been lifesaving advice, such as the principle that the federal government should set national guidelines on hygienic practices and quarantining. I cannot tell which I find more astonishing: that the playbook was ignored, or that no communal outrage emerged upon hearing it was ignored. Poor planning is a major ethical lapse in my opinion. Most charitably, we could call the notion that "someone else will take care of it" magical thinking, but the violation is real. When those with power tacitly expect others to fulfill responsibilities, they abuse that power.

Power dynamics play no small role in the tension between planning and nimbleness. The more power a person has, the nimbler they are allowed to be. The less powerful, the higher the expectation they will stick with the plan. I had a supervisor some years ago who was truly awful at keeping up on email. He made a joke in a public setting about how he knew he was bad at staying on top of his inbox, but that by the time he got around to checking it, he found that problems had solved themselves. I imploded with anger, never letting the smile leave my face as everyone else laughed. I happened to know that the problems were not solving themselves. Other people were solving problems for the leader, overcompensating—sometimes risking policy violations because they were acting beyond their authority—and burning themselves out. He boasted about his nimbleness but was failing in his responsibilities.

Communities need leaders who make good plans and stick with them . . . except for when they should not. Knowing when to stick with the plan, when to improvise, and when to start over, is a form of leadership wisdom that we can cultivate over time while, on a day-to-day basis, holding a healthy tension between planning and nimbleness. The following announcement needs to be one leaders have at the ready if they are going to be good planners who know when plans are not enough: "We had a good plan for how we were going to address X. Then Y became known to us, so we suspended the plan, rethought, regrouped, and here is what we are going to do now . . ."

In a chapter in the anthology *African American Church Leadership* entitled "The Development of a Cohesive Process for Productive Leadership,"[45] Paul Cannings writes about the importance of teamwork in planning. Teamwork does not begin with the creation of a plan; it begins with the leader bringing the team into alignment around shared goals and the vision of the senior minister. He recommends approaching those goals through a multilayered approach that includes personal, spiritual, and organizational adoption of the vision.

The personal layer includes considering how the institution's mission intersects with individual life goals and worldviews. The spiritual connects a group together in the practice of listening for the voice of the Holy Spirit, a person of the Trinity given as a guiding gift. The organizational adoption of the vision might include identifying that which aligns and does not align with the vision, increasing allocation of resources to that which furthers the discerned purpose of the organization. Only then can planning function, he argues, as all are striving for the same objectives.

I come from a tradition in the United Church of Christ that is less clerically centered than traditional African-American Protestant churches. In other words, the authorized leader of the organization is meant to carry out the community's vision, not the other way around. That said, the notion of coming together around a shared purpose transcends churches and is true of any kind of institution, from a family to a corporation. Yet coming together around a shared vision is not tantamount to groupthink or brainwashing. Coming together while still embodying individual wholeness requires a variety of practices that are worthwhile for the sake of human and communal flourishing.

If at this point in this book's exploration of planning versus nimbleness you are saying to yourself, "I don't experience any tension between the two," chances are that you have some work to do yourself. Those who believe themselves excellent planners, who never fail to set the right pace and tone, might be experienced by others as inflexible and unable to listen to others' ideas about process. Those who sense themselves as going with the flow might be causing others around them to overcompensate, taking on stress that should not belong to them. There is no leader who could not improve on their capacities to plan, their abilities to sense when it is time to let a plan go, and balancing those two poles.

NOTES

43. Jack Barentsen, "Pastoral Leadership as Dance: How Embodiment, Practice and Identity Shape Communities and Their Leadership," *Practical Theology: Special themed edition—Embodied Spiritual Practice(s)* 12, no. 3 (2019), http://dx.doi.org/10.1080/1756073X.2019.1591796.

44. Ibid., 312.

45. Paul Cannings, "The Development of a Cohesive Process for Productive Leadership," in June and Mathis, *African American Church Leadership*, 97–104.

12

STRUCTURE VERSUS CREATIVITY

Marks of the leader who is both planful and nimble include the following: they have a goal, they know how to get others on board with and excited about the goal, they can sense when something new and important has come over the transom, and they can set the goal aside or change it accordingly. The tension a leader might sustain between structure and creativity is similar, but distinct. Whereas planning and nimbleness are about direction, structure and creativity are about cognitive style. They relate less to reading situations as they are, and more to a capacity to imagine that which does not yet exist. The structured "wonk" and the creative "artist" are both needed, coexisting in one leader.

Most of us have a default position between the two tensions where we idle, and we learn to shift gears over the course of our lives. In the class I teach on intentional leadership, I ask students at the beginning of each new tension if they can identify their default stance, versus the stance they need to learn. Most students believe they default to creativity over structure. I believe myself to be the opposite. I default to structure and am learning to embrace creativity in my work more as I become secure in my identity as a human being and leader. Structure, frankly, gets a bad rap, and I defend its usefulness.

I initially learned to be a highly structured person as a defense mechanism. I was an extremely outgoing and sometimes awkward child. I felt a strong need to be highly achieving but did not have the kind of intellect that thrived in solitude and interiority. I was not the type to spend hours alone, mastering formulae or reading the classics. Structure gave me the capacity to rein in my big personality and do well in school. I even stated in an interview upon my high school graduation that I credited being organized for most of the good things that had happened to me, saying that organized people get to live more because they have a structure for using their time wisely. I cringe when I read those words, thinking, "Poor kid," but she was not wrong.

Structure is essential for maturation and capacities for creativity. A theme that runs through all three of the tensions described so far is that maturity matters. Considering Kegan's model of adult development yet again, we know that maturity—what his model deems Stage 5—is a both/and state of mind. The tensions themselves rely on the notion that two different things can be true at the same time, and that a singular leader can be in two different frames of mind at once, ready to pivot toward emphasizing one direction over the other as circumstances require.

In Kegan's model, the conical spiral that depicts the extremes between connection and individuality provides an image to describe what Kegan and many others call a "holding environment," touched upon briefly in Chapter 2. A holding environment is a context that feels safe enough for the experimentation necessary for growing up. A holding environment might be a home or a school where acceptance is unconditional and fear of being cast out is minimal to nonexistent. A holding environment is a life-giving, containing structure. A leader who wants a community to evolve and grow needs to create safety through structure. Conversely, the absence of a holding environment might stunt maturation, leaving individuals stuck in radical connectivity (Stage 3) or extreme individualism (Stage 4) unable to find that elusive balance between individual wholeness and communal belonging.

How does a leader create a healthy holding environment? Clear boundaries, understandable expectations, ground rules for engaging others, shared and attainable goals: these are just a few examples of the kinds of structures that cause a community to feel held and thus able to flourish and grow. In a liminal season, the wider culture provides few of these structures. Leaders sometimes, therefore, need to invent them. Structure begets trust, and trust creates a holding environment, and a holding environment makes maturation possible.

As helpful as it is for creating a learning and growing community, structure is not enough for a community to thrive. In an article entitled "Multilayered Leadership: The Christian Leader as Builder, Shepherd, and Gardener,"[46] ministerial leadership scholar Scott Cormode presents a fictional case study on a minister whose town is about to experience a tidal wave of layoffs due to an industrial plant closing. Cormode lays out different scenarios based on three leadership styles. The builder sets forth an action plan. The shepherd keeps the flock together spiritually and emotionally as the community discerns what it must do. The gardener plants theological concepts and scriptural metaphors into conversation, giving the community both resources for making sense of their situation and inspiration for knowing their callings.

A leader who focuses on structure clearly falls into Cormode's category of "builder," and the approach is insufficient on its own. By rushing from event to response, without an in-between step for discernment of the workings and leadings of the Holy Spirit, creativity does not have a fighting chance. Leaders who are all structure and no creativity are likely to make the same mistakes over and over again, as they use the same strategies repeatedly without making room for new possibilities. An overly structured approach to leadership might leave out crucial voices and privilege those in the community who are themselves more comfortable with structure. Many who default to structure do so in part as a response to difficulty managing the anxiety of the community as well as their own anxiety.

The shepherd model, in contrast to the builder model, appears meandering. Although a leader's capacity to stay with the flock emotionally is important—for meeting people where they are is one of the most basic expectations of a relationship between leader and community—communities also look to their leaders for guidance. Barking orders is not ideal, but neither is leaving groups of people to their own devices. I have found myself in many leadership situations where our communities simply did not have time to wander. I was given bad advice early in my career that relational leadership had to happen slowly and quick decision-making was alienating. I have learned over time that a leader can use both builder and shepherd styles at any pace, fast or slow, and that some constituents actually sabotage progress by accusing the leader of not being shepherd-like enough.

I have written previously about the necessary tension between creativity and structure in *Holy Clarity: The Practice of Planning and Evaluation.*[47] In that book, I write about different models for planning programs with a heavy emphasis on structure. I also argue that even the most structure-loving leader needs to infuse communities with creativity and be ready to tear down structures and start over when they inhibit creativity. In *Holy Clarity* I commend three kinds of activities that can unleash creativity in a community: activities that involve the arts; deep, personal sharing; and engagement with those who are different from us. Other practices that might open up space for creativity include retrieving old traditions and making them new, and willingness to cancel or suspend "traditions" that feel draining rather than inspiring.

Structure provides a community with confidence. That confidence should and must be used to try new things and adapt to the demands of the day, not to rest on laurels. Structure also makes it possible to include a wide array of people in a community in leadership roles, which might be the most meaningful way to infuse an institution with creativity.

Consider the common and important leadership task of delegation. When a person with more authority delegates a responsibility to someone with less authority, the temptation might be for the delegator to impose upon the delegate not just a charge for what needs to get done, but controlling and restrictive expectations for exactly how a task might be accomplished. A leader who has struck a healthy tension between structure and creativity instead provides a general framework and vision and then frees the delegate to use their creativity, which is good for everyone. Good for the delegate, because trying to conform to a style not their own is both dehumanizing and unlikely to succeed. Good for the leader, for they receive the full benefit of two heads being better than one. Good for the institution, as creativity spawns more creativity.

Structure provides guardrails and a sense of direction, and creativity makes space for the all-important human element of community life and leadership: people are different from one another, and those differences enrich communities. In a chapter titled "Mobilizing and Motivating Congregational Effectiveness" in the anthology *African American Church Leadership*, Lloyd Blue writes that the leader should dedicate significant energy to presenting and reinforcing core values, such as mission-mindedness or servant leadership.[48] Then, the leader should focus on bringing together the right leaders and training them well. Finally, the leader needs to let people do their work. By empowering those recruits, rather than restricting their creativity through insistence on constant permission-seeking or control over implementation styles, their creativity belongs to the whole community. We can take from Blue's argument the following guidance: (1) the right leaders, (2) trained well, (3) furnished with a clear vision for which to strive, and (4) given meaningful opportunities and important decisions to make, enrich the community and lead to high levels of satisfaction for all.

So far, this exploration of the tension one must sustain between structure and creativity has suggested that too much attention to structure can be suffocating for new ideas. A similar risk exists with an overemphasis on creativity over structure or the suggestion that structure is the enemy of creativity: the risk being death to emergence. Beaumont argues, as described previously,[49] that the leader's role and responsibility in a liminal time is to prevent the community from going back to old ways by making them comfortable enough with uncertainty that they do not rush to closure amidst unknowing. That which we might become after a time of in-betweenness will emerge. We cannot force it. We can, however, create situations where the anxiety of unknowing is too much for a community.

I am what an administrative leadership professional might describe as a "process person." This means that I map processes out with some care rather than allowing all dimensions of group work to emerge. For instance, I have a specific approach to short-term task forces my board and I convene for short-term initiatives, such as creating a new program or refreshing a strategic plan:

1. Convene a task force constituted of appropriate stakeholders with varied perspectives.

2. Bring the group together for discussion that helps them get to know each other and the mandate.

3. Break the group into small task forces of two or three that work on deliverables between meetings.

4. Listen to those task forces, using their input to write a preliminary set of recommendations.

5. Give the preliminary set of recommendations to the whole task force for review.

6. Revise recommendations and submit them on behalf of the task force to the governing body.

Seems controlling, right? Seems routinized, right? And yet people who serve on task forces I convene tend to have good experiences, where they report that they felt their time *and their wisdom* was used well. A process with too much structure will squelch wisdom-sharing. An efficient process need not do so.

Cormode privileges and commends a "gardener" style of leadership most of all. As stated previously, Cormode writes a story—which might or might not be based on reality—about a congregation located near a factory that will soon close down, putting many congregants and town residents out of work. Cormode depicts three ways a meeting might go in the immediate aftermath of the news of the factory's closure. In "builder" mode, the minister facilitates discussion among church leaders about what the congregation as a whole will do to provide support for those in need. In the "shepherd" mode, the minister allows ideas and energies to emerge without guiding them in any particular direction. The "gardener" model presents a minister who plants theological seeds in an emergency meeting in the form of providing biblical metaphors for the situation, and those participating in the meeting adopt those metaphors and cultivate their growth onto a plan of action.

Providing metaphors unleashes creativity, where people can see their circumstances from a different vantage point, and thus imagine new possibilities for next steps. In his later book *Making Spiritual Sense: Christian Leaders as Spiritual Interpreters,*[50] Cormode expands this idea, arguing that the primary role of the religious leader is to interpret the world using theological lenses and language, freeing the community to enact its interpretation of God's imagination.

Consider this example: on January 6, 2021, the school I serve carried out a carefully planned worship service for Epiphany. I can say it was "carefully planned" because it was planned twice: before rioters stormed the US Capitol, and after.

The worship leadership team responsible for the service, comprised of two students, had an order for an Epiphany service in hand and ready to go when the news blew up with terrifying images of people with guns and Confederate flags storming the Capitol. When student and senior leaders met to decide what to do, the students' temptation was to throw the structure out the window, but I persuaded them not to. Everyone in the nation was rattled by events in Washington, DC, and because the service was taking place less than four hours after those events began, I believed it unlikely that many would have coherent thoughts to share in an open prayer service. I encouraged the leadership to work within the framework they had already chosen, with an addition or subtraction here and there. The result was a structure that caused the community to feel held and safe, and the times of open sharing brought out brilliant new perspectives that caused all to know the Holy Spirit had entered the space with us.

Too often, people view structure as creativity's enemy: not so. Yet there is a difference between *structure* that creates a holding environment and *control* that inhibits individuality, risk-taking, and freedom to follow the movement of the Holy Spirit. Structure, held in tension with creativity, causes new ideas to flourish.

Unlike other tensions described in this book, the two named in this section are not created equal. Creativity matters more. Structure without the free flow of ideas quickly descends into controlling behaviors on the part of leaders, who in turn descend into demagoguery. Structure serves creativity; the reverse is not true. Protecting every person's right to creative and imaginative thinking is a key purpose of structure. Structure is the scaffold upon which the workers stand as they build the cathedral; it is not the cathedral itself. As described previously, creativity, especially as it is expressed by a community rather than an individual, relies on structure to set it free and move it from inside the mind out into the world.

For all these reasons, leaders must monitor the tension between creativity and structure with an eye on how structure is either enhancing or inhibiting creativity. When is creativity threatened because we do not have enough structure? When is it threatened because we have too much structure, or the wrong kind of structure? We also must make conscious choices to insert creativity into processes' structure, recognizing that group process can be fun when it includes creativity, and it can be dull and oppressive when it does not.

An illustration of a leadership practice that blends structure and creativity is the use of "World Café"–style large-group gatherings. I will close this chapter describing how to organize one. When a large group needs to deliberate over a question together, a World Café is one way to break up stale patterns for gathering, such as plenary style meetings where people take turns sharing opinions. In a World Café, the leader frames a guiding question and sets up a space where the group will gather as though in a café.

Each table is covered with newsprint, and each table has supplies for drawing. Food and drink lay at the outskirts of the space. Everyone is invited to fill their cups and plates, choose a table, and then each table discusses the guiding question while snacking, drawing, talking, and listening. Every few minutes—fifteen? twenty?—the leader invites people to change tables and continue the conversation with a different collection of people. At the end of an hour or so, the newsprint moves from table to wall, and the café becomes an art gallery. The drawings become the "minutes" of the meeting.

A World Café is a particularly helpful way to gather a multi-generational group. Neither very young nor very old people are going to feel immediately comfortable with the format; it is bound to be new for everyone. Boundaries between visual versus auditory learners break down, as do hierarchies. The event requires planning, organization, management, and instruction: in other words, structure. That structure sets creativity free and puts it to work in an organization visioning a new future toward which it can strive.

NOTES

46. Scott Cormode, "Multilayered Leadership: The Christian Leader as Builder, Shepherd, and Gardener," *The Journal of Religious Leadership* 1, no. 2 (2002): 69–104.

47. Drummond, *Holy Clarity*.

48. Lloyd Blue, "Mobilizing and Motivating the Congregation for Effectiveness," in June and Mathis, *African American Church Leadership*, 105–16.

49. Beaumont, *How to Lead When You Don't Know Where You're Going*.

50. Scott Cormode, *Making Spiritual Sense: Christian Leaders as Spiritual Interpreters* (Eugene, OR: Wipf & Stock, 2006).

AFFILIATIVE VERSUS AUTHORITATIVE LEADERSHIP STYLES

One great irony of Christian ministerial leadership is this: God is one, and God's Truth is one, but in order to function in human community we need to be more than one thing. Only God is fully and utterly consistent, and we get glimpses into God's will through the Gospel. We know that God is love and wants us to love each other. We know that life wins, every time, in God's realm. Early Christian theologian Augustine described a "City of God," where coexisting with all that is happening around us is a separate and perfect plane, best described as God's imagination for creation.[51] The work of the Christian is to live in this fallen world and keep our eyes on the City of God, seeking out every opportunity to cause the world to resemble the City of God more. In order to achieve that project, human beings cannot be perfectly consistent. They must adapt enough to the fallen world to aid in its transformation. On the surface, what appears to be inconsistency is simply a necessity of leadership in a complex world that is not yet what it needs to be.

Consider Kegan's developmental model. Throughout our lives, we oscillate between radical dependence (infancy's dependence on the parent, adolescence's dependency on what others think) and independence (the toddler's adamant "no!" and the young adult's self-discovery). Ultimately, the mature individual blends internal wholeness with full connection with the community. They are not one half of a whole when in a relationship, nor are they along for the emotional ride in a community. They embody Rabbi Edwin Friedman's ideal of separateness-yet-connectedness,[52] both at once.

To embody two things at once is not hypocrisy, disingenuousness, or saying what people want to hear; it is a mark of mature adulthood. That said, the outward behaviors of a hypocrite, and the adult balancing two realities at once, are not always easily distinguishable, which is why we all should avoid judging leaders hastily and harshly for appearing to "flipflop." God is consistent, as is God's truth; human beings adapt and change as they mature, and as circumstances evolve.

The final tension to be described in this chapter relates to leadership style. Having spent a career exploring the concept that intelligence is multiple, not monolithic, and not related to cognition alone, Dan Goleman writes about how leaders both possess and can adopt various leadership styles, depending on their gifts as well as the circumstances in which they lead. He zeroes in on six styles, and this chapter will explore two in particular.[53]

Here is Goleman's full collection of categories of leadership styles:

- Coercive leaders demand compliance.
- Authoritative leaders mobilize people toward a vision.
- Affiliative leaders create emotional bonds and harmony.
- Democratic leaders build consensus.
- Pacesetting leaders model and expect excellence and self-direction.
- Coaching leaders develop people for the future.

At first glance, one might think that, except for the first style—coercion—all styles named are wholly positive and worthy. Goleman makes a persuasive argument, however, that each of these styles has its benefits and detriments, all depending upon the context and the goal. For instance, even a coercive leader can be right for an institution at a certain moment, say, when it is moving in a decidedly unwise or unjust direction. Pacesetting leaders might inspire, but they might also fail to provide adequate clarity about expectations while rushing ahead, expecting others to follow. None of the styles is perfect, yet each of them is right for certain situations.

The two styles I argue are most commonly employed and important for ministerial leaders are the *authoritative* and *affiliative* styles, and it is between them that leaders must strike a balance and establish tension. The authoritative leader works with a community to cast a vision, create a plan to achieve the vision, and then motivate the community to carry out the plan. When saboteurs living out some unhealthy need attempt to disrupt and derail the plan, the authoritative leader decisively pushes past the saboteur on behalf of that which the community has embraced. When resistance is meaningful and thoughtful, the authoritative leader uses convening power to revisit the vision and plan and make changes as needed, including possibly suspending the direction or choosing a new one. The authoritative leader by no means works alone, but they do take charge.

Affiliative leadership begins with relationships. The affiliative leader takes pains to meet with constituents and colleagues alike one-on-one during ordinary times so that relationships are solid when storms come. They are unafraid to get to know their communities, building meaningful connections rooted in love. Affiliative leaders lead through being radically present and attuned to their communities. They are so in touch with the community that they are able to sense its yearned-for direction and shepherd it using that intuited trajectory as a guide.

The downsides of an authoritative leadership style are multiple. It can veer into coercion when the authoritative leader mistakes meaningful resistance for sabotage and neglects important concerns en route to the goal. Second, the authoritative leader can veer into pacesetting and get far out ahead of the community. This happens initially when a community trusts that the authoritative leader is so motivated, so on top of it, that they do not have to be. The community might come together around a vision but then disengage and allow the authoritative leader to do all the work and take all the heat. The authoritative leader fails to sustain communal ownership for the selected direction and does not include the rest of the community in small victories along the way. The consequences of the community pulling back and allowing the authoritative leader to do the work are twofold: leadership burnout and loss of buy-in.

Contrary to popular opinion, professional burnout results not from working too hard, but from working under unrealistic expectations. Consider the student who enrolls in school full-time while also working full-time: burnout is likely, because there are only so many hours in the day. Consider the social worker whose caseload doubles with no change to the expectations of the services they will provide: again, the number of duties is a problem, but it is the impossible standards for success that will lead to burnout. Authoritative leaders are vulnerable to burnout when the leaders around them pull back and "allow" them to run the show. Why? Because no matter how authoritative a style one might have, a leader can only carry out the tasks for which they have been granted authority. They cannot do others' work for them and succeed, for they will either burn out, curry resentment from others, or both.

I have long believed that buy-in receives insufficient attention in ministerial leadership. In school leadership, the expression "buy-in" rolls off the tongue and is considered a precious resource to be cultivated and cherished. Leaders generate buy-in for new ideas by carefully bringing stakeholders along to the point where they not only accept new ideas but embrace and take part in shaping them. Moving forward with a new initiative without sufficient buy-in dooms the initiative to fail, no matter how much power the one spearheading the initiative might have.

Buy-in is something affiliative leaders gather easily. Sometimes, affiliative leaders move forward without doing enough to communicate, cajole, and involve others, and those others simply let them do so because they are focused on other things and simply not interested enough to resist. Those who have not bought in might allow the authoritative leader to have what they seem to want, but in time, that lack of investment will be the new idea's downfall—be it an initiative, a program, an institutional direction, or even a whole institution.

Maintaining balance between authoritative and affiliative leadership is the best way to temper the authoritative leader's tendency to blow past people. By caring about relationships, authoritative leaders enter administrative processes surrounded by people whom they know well enough to read, and whom they trust to ask for input and advice. Furthermore, if the leader has done a good job creating two-way relationships with constituents, they will receive either direct or indirect feedback regarding whether their new ideas are any good, and on how to best communicate that which they are trying to achieve. Rather than making their way far out in front of the community, they stay together with their people, enough so that they do not take on the work of others, which can lead to burnout. They build buy-in using channels of communication that they have been creating and strengthening since well before a new idea was even on the table.

Given how important it is for the authoritative leader to infuse their style with the affiliative practices of building and leading from relationships, why bother with the authoritative style at all? Why not lead in an affiliative way all the time? First, affiliative leaders at times lack direction because they are so busy cultivating bonds that the institution's mission takes a secondary position. As missional stewards, leaders who put relationships ahead of mission all the time might fall short in fulfilling their responsibilities. Second, Goleman writes that affiliative leaders tend to tolerate mediocrity, focusing on nurture of individuals over motivation of teams. Authoritative leadership provides an important counterbalance, in that leaders can sense when to demonstrate compassion and understanding, yet they can also sense when compassion has veered into territory where the mission of the organization might be receding into the background.

The tension between affiliative and authoritative styles of leadership raises many questions related to the nature of power dynamics. Here are just a few examples of such questions, when one considers how this tension plays out in context:

- When might an authoritative leader either come across as, or actually function like, a coercive one?

- When might affiliative leadership come across as, or actually function as, weakness?

- How might the societal position of the leader—gender, race, ability, sexual orientation, national origin, stature, and size— require attention when dialing up and dialing down affiliative and authoritative styles?

Goleman entitles an article summarizing his theoretical framework, "Leadership That Gets Results." An even deeper critique of his model might raise questions about goal orientation in leadership styles. When does "getting results" tend toward utilitarianism that treats people like machines or cogs in a machine?

Looking back over all five of the tensions described in this chapter, one could pose many analogous questions. When does veering too far in one direction or the other cause damage? How do human differences and the power dynamics resulting from them play a role? The reason I use the term "tension" over the term "balance," although both words do appear throughout the chapter, is that "tension" suggests ongoing thoughtfulness and self-examination. A balance can be struck and then ignored as long as it is sustained. Tension requires ongoing effort; tension calls for attention. With each new situation, with each new discovery of the ethical implications of leadership, with every way in which we grow and mature, we need a new investigation of how to achieve balance in the tensions named in this chapter. The work is meaningful, and it is never done.

The tension we must strike between creativity and structure is particularly relevant to affiliative versus authoritative leadership styles. When leaders want to free a community's creativity, they might be tempted to lean on their affiliative relationships, but what is often needed is a structure that can serve as a vessel for the creativity of others.

Consider this example: in February of 2021, a small group of students emailed me wanting to start a newsletter on music and spirituality for our community. They wanted us to pay them to create it and cover all the expenses associated with it. I brought the idea to my staff team, and all of us agreed that our community was "newslettered out." We were expanding our program-wide newsletter to include a devotional every week, and the wider divinity school was creating a weekly news piece, seeking to respond to student feedback that the pandemic had them feeling disconnected. I replied to the email, thanked the students who made the proposal, and explained the bigger picture. I declined to approve their proposal with much appreciation for their having taken initiative.

Two days later, I received an email back. It was many paragraphs in length and began with euphemisms like "surprised and disappointed" that told me the students were hurt by my having shot down their idea. I realized my rookie mistake: these are my students, not a marketing company making a pitch. They reached out with an idea. I should have met with them, heard them out, and talked the idea through. Maybe I would have seen through new eyes and changed my mind. Or maybe not; that is not the point. I needed to put relationships over programs in that moment. Therefore, I created a new moment, asked for the meeting; a do-over. It did not go well.

Students were feeling defensive, and I did not like their idea much more in person than I had on paper. We found a way through, however, with a compromise pilot project where they will produce a small, set number of newsletters which we will then evaluate together. It was only a few days later when I went to my staff with a different kind of question. I had noticed that some of our students have been unusually chummy with me lately. Usually, I like chummy. I invite them to call me by my first name, which is for me a matter of polity and theology, and I publish my cell phone number. Of course, I do not pick up my cell phone at all hours. I use voicemail to moderate the inflow of correspondence and do not respond to messages when I am not working, except in emergencies. But "emergency" is in the eye of the beholder; is it not? We are in the midst of a pandemic and a season of cultural clash over racism and politics. These days, everything feels like a crisis.

Such was the case when a student texted me during a difficult moment in the evening, and I called him to check in. The next day, I was asking my team, "I could use some feedback on the way I'm managing my boundaries during this strange, distanced season." I explained what had happened and they had some useful feedback. They also reminded me that this is everyone's first pandemic. We are all learning on the job about what kind of boundaries maintain our hoped-for connectedness while maintaining a healthy separation that helps everyone.

The two implications for practice that emerge from these illustrations are these: keep an eye on sustaining an authoritative presence and take care of relationships too. Do not expect to get it exactly right, ever, and do not be afraid to ask for advice on improvement. Request second chances when you need them to reset the relationship. As mentioned previously, these two leadership styles I commend as the ones most relevant to ministerial leadership, affiliative versus authoritative leadership, are subject to numerous cultural factors. Constituents find my affiliative style more acceptable than my authoritative style due to my gender. Black constituents do not always know what to make of my affiliative side due to my whiteness: they wonder if I am genuine or, like so many others they have encountered, likely to draw them in, let them down, and hurt them.

Authenticity thus becomes the important plumbline holding these two styles in tension.

Ultimately, authentic commitment to a mission (the authoritative engine) and authentic concern for each individual member of the community (the affiliative instinct) feed into one another. Members of a community or team can sense that their leader cares about them, and that makes them want to pursue the mission more vigorously. They then develop a personal connection to the mission, which makes them more motivated to transcend their individual concerns and strive to achieve that which the community has set out to do, sometimes embodying an authoritative leadership style of their own. Working together, affiliative leadership styles increase buy-in, and buy-in promotes mission focus, and mission focus characterizes an authoritative leadership style.

NOTES

51. Augustine of Hippo, *The City of God* (Washington, DC: Catholic University of America Press, 2008).

52. Friedman, *A Failure of Nerve*.

53. Daniel Goleman, *Leadership That Gets Results* (Cambridge, MA: Harvard Business Review Classics, 2017).

IMPLICATIONS FOR PRACTICE AND CONCLUSION

When considering all five of these tensions, and what they have in common, three habits emerge that one could call the marks of an intentional leader. First, the intentional leader moves from trees, to forest, and back to trees regularly over the course of the day, even over the course of one event or meeting. They consider the individuals in the community, and the community as a whole, without becoming obsessed with one or the other. They consider the vision—the big picture—and how they are carrying out their daily duties—the little picture—either at the same time or in rapid alternation. They cultivate close relationships with their teammates while also setting boundaries that make it possible to keep their eyes on the mission. Zoom in; zoom out; repeat.

Second, intentional leaders understand how crucial it is to choose good leaders and empower them. In business settings, one sometimes hears expressions like, "Hire slowly; fire quickly." Leaders must lift up other leaders who have promise for success and with whom they work effectively and easily; the challenges of communal leadership are hard enough without the wrong raw materials. In religious organizations, this challenge is particularly difficult. Many or most of the leadership is made up of volunteers, and the temptation is to promote those who care the most, rather than those who would be most effective. One learns through experience, however, that thanking a person for their commitment by empowering them to a role where they will not succeed, drive everyone crazy, or both: this is not good leadership. Setting people up to fail is no favor to anyone, including the one who is lifted up into a leadership role that does not match their gifts.

Finally, intentional leaders say yes and no to invitations and opportunities decisively. They can assess quickly whether a new opportunity fits with their institution's mission or their own priorities because they are not only highly attuned to mission but understand how quickly distractions can undermine their quality of life and their effectiveness. They are slow to institutionalize new ideas into programs, starting with experiments and pilot initiatives that test for viability and relevance. When a new initiative that seemed like a good idea at its inception is no longer working, they are quick to let go of it. When they hire a new team member, they both invest heavily in onboarding and supervisory support and build in a three-month probationary period after which evaluation can result in showing that new team member the door. Do those practices run counter to each other? No. They must be held in tension.

These disciplines of saying yes decisively, entering new commitments feet first, and letting go of that which does not work, result from maintaining healthy tensions that keep leaders attuned to the needs of the community. That attunement improves what one might mistake for instincts, but which is really a sophisticated and deep understanding of the organization's mission and the needs of those who make the organization up. "Yes" can be said with joy, and "no" without guilt or remorse, because the right answer is obvious to the one highly sensitive to what the organization needs, or what the leaders themselves need to flourish. Moving from the balcony to the dance floor and back again, seeking out good raw material in every potential partner in leadership, and saying yes and no with the mission in mind: these practical steps help leaders strike the balance they need and are each rooted in concepts to which one could refer as "intentional leadership." In the introduction I use the metaphor of the sewing machine to illustrate the concept of energizing tensions that pull against one another in a way that promotes strength and integrity. A sewing machine requires light tension between the thread coming down from the top and the thread coming up from the bobbin below. If the tension is off in either direction, the garment will not hold together. If it is too tight, the threads will snap, and if it is too loose, they will become tangled. Religious leadership across different kinds of institutions requires continuous moderation of tension. All kinds of leadership—religious and otherwise—are studies in contrasts, juxtaposition, and balance. For instance, a leader needs to be warm and inviting, but not a pushover. The leader must strive with gusto, but over-functioning is bad for the health of both leader and institution. A faith community must be stable and sustainable but sometimes must go out on a limb for the sake of what is right.

The previous chapters named and defined five tensions. This chapter will lift up two bodies of theory: community organizing and large-group dynamics. In liminal seasons, leaders cannot expect old theoretical frameworks to serve as motivators. Even relatively recent theories, like the change theories about which I have written extensively, seem to have lost their capacity to clarify what needs to be done and energize leaders and their communities. Why? Because change theory relies on a vision, and casting a vision into the future feels even more like an imaginary exercise now than it might have a year or two ago.

Already, when the pandemic descended, much was in chaos. Political polarization was becoming scarier by the day, and the US was both isolating itself internationally and picking fights with historical allies. White supremacy was on the rise, and it was becoming more and more clear that the President of the United States was all for it, at least insofar as he was benefitting from it. Having a plan, however, was still possible. And then, suddenly, it was not.

Covid-19 called upon leaders to set aside plans that relied on a future focus, and day after day, I witnessed and heard stories of profound exhaustion. We blamed the exhaustion on too many hours on Zoom, with many working from home while also caring for children, and no doubt we were partially right. Extroverts had lost their primary energizing source: time spent in close proximity with others, feeding off the energy of others. Introverts still needed to connect with others over technology and safe social distance to do their work, so they did not get to recharge their batteries on their own terms. Essential workers had no choice in the matter and had to endure the anxiety of possible exposure to a frightening infectious agent.

I leaned heavily on what I know about change leadership, program planning and evaluation, and emotional systems during those early days. Eventually, however, I needed a guide that did not rely on a future vision, because the future was too uncertain. I wrote this book during the Covid-19 pandemic. During those months, which turned into years, I made precious few plans that did not at some point require significant revision. I worked with colleagues to reorganize the way we teach, worship, plan, budget, raise money, spend money, supervise, and think together. At times I felt like I was building sandcastles and just waiting for the tide to come in and wash them away. Now, nothing in me wants to pull out the old playbook, as I will not soon trust a future vision as the primary source of my leadership motivation again.

Leaders working amidst a liminal time crave structure and patterns, whether they know it or not. They get advice about fitness, sleep hygiene, and diet, but little guidance or conventional wisdom are available for guiding leaders in how they use their time or assess the expenditure of their own human resources. Intentional leadership seeks to provide practical and specific advice on how leaders can strike and maintain a tension that can energize them, even when goals are unavailable as a motivator, given the future's uncertainty.

Consider the following illustration in the form of a fictional case, "Lost in Space":

The First Congregational Church of Norrington has more space than it can handle. Given its urban location, one might think of physical space as an asset. Rents are high in the neighborhood where the church is located, and many businesses would be happy to have such a central location with both good foot traffic and a parking lot. In contrast, clergy and lay leaders at FCCN have long felt overwhelmed by the responsibilities that come with the space. At every monthly meeting, the church's lay leaders—or "council"—devote more than half their time to issues with the building.

The church's minister, Estelle, has encouraged the council to bring in a consultant to help them to figure out a better way to manage their space, both logistically and psychologically. Relatively new to her role, and succeeding a predecessor who was quick to take action without consultation, Estelle wanted to get the council's input before bringing in professional assistance, thus providing a model for what it means to share leadership. The church's leadership team has therefore contracted with Adrian, a nonprofit management consultant, to assess their situation and help them to come up with new options for the future. Adrian sent the following preliminary report:

> I began work with FCCN by visiting a church council meeting and interviewing those present about the issues that caused them to contact me. After a ninety-minute consultation, I took note of the following issues:
>
> 1. No one on the council likes the idea of renting space to for-profit entities in the wider community just for the sake of making money.
>
> 2. Similarly, none is interested in segmenting the building and selling parts of it "condominium style," as the church's architecture and layout aren't given to easily break sections of the facility apart.
>
> 3. Renting to other nonprofits would require staff attention to the various responsibilities that come with leasing property, and such staff support isn't currently available.
>
> 4. Members of the congregation like having freedom to use any part of the building, whenever they wish, and they hesitate to give that freedom up.
>
> 5. Given the building's urban location, members of the council expressed concern about security issues if the

building were to be opened up more to the wider community.

6. The more the wider community uses the building, the more quickly it becomes worn down and in need of cleaning and renovation, but the building's perceived emptiness feels wasteful, not to mention depressing.

After the council meeting, I scheduled individual conversations with members of the church's staff, including the custodian and administrative assistant. The custodian was negative about the idea of rethinking use of the church space, believing that it would be taken for granted that her work would increase without commensurate compensation. The administrator was more open to the possibility, but he shared the concern about more responsibility without added resources.

The pastor's and my one-on-one conversation made clear that the space issues that led FCCN to contract with me relate to a wider concern about the church's present and future. Estelle has served FCCN for just over one year. She was familiar with the church for many years before taking the new call, and she had wondered what more could be done for the church to leverage its location. Upon beginning her work, she learned that many—even most—members of the congregation do not live in the city or neighborhood where the church building is located. They live in surrounding towns but consider FCCN to be their urban foothold and an excuse to visit the city and see friends there.

Those members were hesitant sometimes to visit the urban center themselves, Estelle said, given dense traffic and some crime, let alone to open the sanctuary more to the neighborhood. When I asked Estelle if she had shared the concern with the congregation, she demurred. She is still new enough that she wants to get a sense of the congregation's desires and calling, so she was still in what she called "observation mode."

Some basic research about the neighborhood in which the church is located has demonstrated dramatic demographic shifts in the surrounding area over the past fifty years. Soaring real estate costs pushed some member families to relocate. Those moving to the area appear to be at more transitory points in their lives, not necessarily seeking a church home in that they are not thinking about a lifelong commitment to the area. Some neighbors do express, however, a desire to build community in the area, given that it remains highly residential rather than commercial with few public and shared spaces to congregate.

The church finances are sustainable for the time being, due to a combination of giving and investments, but the church's finances lack connection with a mission or vision statement. Recommendation #1: church leaders should cast a vision for the church's future, and then consider how the building could help the church live into that vision. I cannot offer further recommendations until that first one is taken into consideration.

Yours truly, Adrian

Members of the council read Adrian's consultation report and gathered to discuss it. First, members pressed Estelle. Why, they asked, did she tell the consultant observations she hadn't shared with them directly? She had similar questions for them: why had they told Adrian six reasons why nothing could change, when they'd hired Adrian to recommend changes? After the group vented frustration on each other, they turned their frustration to Adrian: "Is he basically going on strike until we can tell him our vision for our church's future?" Their frustration quickly gave way, however, to understanding of Adrian's predicament. Adrian couldn't tell them what to want, only how to get what they want with the help of the asset of the church's property.

The council decided to take two major steps in answering Adrian's key question about the church's vision. First, some members of the council created a survey with the following questions:

- What constitutes a true member of FCCN? What access to the building does a person require to understand themselves to be true members?

- Who are our neighbors and partners? Whom are we called to serve through use of the asset that is our building?

- Who should be in charge of determining how, and by whom, the building is used?

- What concerns do you have about coordination of building use? Upkeep of the building?

- What creative ideas do you have for making fuller use of the building?

Analyzed survey results demonstrated that most members of the congregation wanted the space to be available to likeminded partners in the area. Respondents stated that, logistics aside, sharing the space generously and hospitably would be their preference. Some came up with creative ideas for potential partners in the neighborhood. Others suggested that monetizing parts of the building would likely be a good investment given dwindling membership and philanthropy, but any revenue should be reinvested in making the church building widely available to the community. One or two stated concern that the church staff should not be expected to take on new projects without training and compensation.

With survey results in hand, the council's second step was to call together a congregational conversation to discuss what they learned. Some conflict emerged early in the meeting, because members not on the council were unaware of any necessity for a conversation about space use. The council had not shared widely how much time and attention the building was taking, with so little return on investment from that time as related to the life of the congregation. Three members spoke out in favor of going with the flow, following the will of the Spirit, and simply letting the *status quo* continue. Some council members got a tad flustered: "We want to go with the flow, too, but we need you to help us figure out a direction, as this facility comes with a lot of responsibility."

The stalemate was broken when a respected long-time member of FCCN offered up some prophetic words: "When I first started worshiping here, I lived around the corner, and I thought it was a gift that the church was here for the neighborhood. It was a gift I received. Now that I live a twenty-minute drive away, I think of the church building not so much as a gift I receive, but as one I want to give, even if the church's neighbors aren't my geographical neighbors anymore."

Estelle and the chair of the council crafted an email to Adrian together, which said, "We think we're ready. We want to get your advice on how to gradually turn our facility into a community center for the neighborhood. Our members want access to it, of course, but as one among many groups who use it. How can we structure such an arrangement financially and legally? What new resources would we need, and what allies would we need in the neighborhood to start down this road?" Adrian wrote back, "I'm on it." *Fin.*

One could imagine many ways in which the "sewing exercise" could help the congregation's leaders to assess their actions and effectiveness in the process of discerning best use of its space. Imagine, at the end of their consulting project, that Adrian helped the church council to reflect on how they handled the process of discerning a new way to think about their building. They could use the grid below to analyze the way they dwelt in, and then emerged from, liminality.

This exercise could take place in a council meeting. It could serve Estelle in her private reflections on where she succeeded and what she might consider next time. Notice that the evaluation of tensions does not focus on meeting the goal, although the goal was indeed met in this fictional case. Amidst a liminal time, getting the process basically right by bringing a community together around a relevant and important question often has to be success enough.

This book presents the idea that goal-oriented leadership, with a plumbline "out there" in an unknown future, is insufficient guidance for leaders in a liminal time. Disciplined leadership is important, as it helps leaders to feel satisfied even when conventional marks of success—getting goals checked off a list—are not achievable. Throughout the book, I have alternated examples between faith communities and other types of missional organizations, with "missional" meaning that improving the world is a primary objective. Beyond "missional," however, what makes disciplined, intentional leadership specifically and inherently Christian?

Individuality	*Community*
Each individual voice, from Estelle to the longtime member who broke the stalemate, was taken seriously and included in decision-making.	Church leaders engaged an inclusive process that blended external and internal voices, as well as a concern for external and internal constituents.
Inclusivity	*Clear identity*
The council invited many voices into their process, both internal and external. Church leaders and members grasped the importance of full participation in the neighborhood rather than privileging members as related to building use.	The council took seriously that, even though members were not invited to think of the church's facility as a "clubhouse," they had every right to feeling entitled to a say in its use.
Planning	*Nimbleness*
Estelle saw the pattern of how much energy the building was requiring of the congregation's leaders, and rather than try to "stop talking about it," she encouraged making a new plan.	The council was flexible enough to bring in and listen to a consultant. Similarly, they brainstormed with the congregation.
Structure	*Creativity*
Bringing in a consultant who conducted interviews, carrying out a survey, calling together a forum: all of these actions served as scaffolding to a new way of thinking about space.	The council opened itself up to a wide variety of possibilities for their space.
Affiliative leadership	*Authoritative leadership*
Estelle refused to follow in the footsteps of her predecessors, who over-functioned. Perhaps, however, she played the "I'm new" card too readily when she could instead have said "I'm listening."	The council did not take the bait when members of the congregation expressed hope that a decision might be put off indefinitely, "going with the flow" at the expense of leaders' sanity and the congregation's mission.

The Christian faith is well-versed in what it means to be in between times. Much of the Hebrew Bible describes stories of wandering and waiting, and life did not stop during those seasons, nor did God abandon creation amidst liminality. When Jesus died and was raised from the dead and then ascended into heaven, his followers expected that he would return imminently, and they lived accordingly. In order to live amidst in-betweenness, Christians need to live like disciples, and their leaders must disciple them.

A disciple of Christ wanders but is not lost. A disciple is utterly free, but not free to do... whatever. The disciple is free to *follow Jesus* however their spirit and heart calls. Jesus was a savior of the present moment. He chastened those whose so-called goals had distracted them from following him. He taught them to tether their actions to that which was called for by an ethic of love. Intentional leadership keeps us in the present moment, and it is in that moment where Jesus finds us and shows us the way to a new kind of success that transcends what we can fully understand.

In the words of the prophet Isaiah (43:19a), God is "about to do a new thing; now it springs forth, do you not perceive it?" Those who perceive it are present, and intentional leadership is what puts and keeps us in a disciple's frame of mind: attentive, active, and ready.